Skills for

MODERN WORLD HISTORY

GCSE History Companions

Other history titles by Philip Sauvain:

Hulton New Histories:
  1 Tribes and Tribunes
  2 Serf and Crusader
  3 Crown and Parliament
  4 Forge and Factory
  5 War and Peace
  Teacher's Book

British Economic and Social History – Book 1 1700–1870
                                                  Book 2 1850–present day

GCSE History Companions:
  Skills for British Economic and Social History
  Skills for British and European History

Modern World History – 1919 onwards

European and World History – 1815–1919

Lively History:
  Town and Country – 1485–1789
  Empire, City and Industry – 1789–1901
  Conflict, Science and Society: The Twentieth Century

Further history titles from Stanley Thornes and Hulton include:

Kelly: *A World of Change: Britain in the Early Modern Age 1450–1700*
  World of Change Topic Books:
    A City at War: Oxford 1642–46
    Elizabeth & Akbar: Portraits of Power
    Scolding Tongues: The Persecution of 'Witches'
    Bare Ruined Choirs: The Fate of a Welsh Abbey
    Exploring Other Civilisations
    Children in Tudor England
    The Cromwell Family
    To the New World: The Founding of Pennsylvania

Leeds: *Peace and War: A First Source Book*

Whiting (series co-ordinator): *Footprints:*
  Industry
  The Countryside
  Towns
  Churches

Archer & Shepley: *Witnessing History* (Oral history for GCSE)

Whiting: *Crime and Punishment: A Study Across Time*
      (Study book and Teacher's Resource book)

Simpson: *Changing Horizons: Britain 1914–1980*

Simpson: *Working with Sources: Case Studies in Twentieth Century History*

Skills for

MODERN WORLD HISTORY

GCSE History Companions

PHILIP SAUVAIN

STANLEY THORNES (PUBLISHERS) LTD

Text © Philip Sauvain, 1988

First published in 1988 by:
Stanley Thornes (Publishers) Ltd
Old Station Drive
Leckhampton
CHELTENHAM GL53 0DN
England

Reprinted 1989

British Library Cataloguing in Publication Data

Sauvain, Philip, *1933–*
    Skills for modern world history: GCSE
    history companion.
    1. England. Secondary schools. Curriculum
    subjects: History. Study techniques
    I. Title
    907'.1242

    ISBN 0–85950–826–9

Cover illustration: Churchill, Roosevelt and Stalin at the Yalta Conference in February 1945. Standing directly behind them are, from left to right, Anthony Eden, Edward Stettinius, Sir Alexander Cadogan, Viachislay Molotov and Averill Harriman. Reproduced by kind permission of the trustees of the Imperial War Museum, London.

Typeset by Tech-Set, Gateshead, Tyne & Wear
in 10½/12½ Times
Printed and bound in Great Britain at The Bath Press, Avon

Contents

Acknowledgements

The author and publishers are grateful to the following for supplying and giving permission to reproduce illustrative material:

Associated Press, pages 87, 89 (below), 98, 117, 126; BBC, page 50; BBC Hulton Picture Library pages 13, 20, 59 (above), 84, 101 (right); Rudolf Barten/Cologne Tourist Office, page 106 (right); Bilderdienst, page 64 (above); British Library, pages 28, 80; Bundesarchiv, pages 19, 27; Daily Mail for extracts from the *Daily Chronicle* and *Daily Mail*, page 59; Daily Telegraph, page 82; Edimedia, page 65; Fitzroy Collection, page 66 (below); Greater London Photograph Library, page 37; Illustrated London News, page 115 (below); Imperial War Museum, pages 42, 62, 77 (above), 79, 104 (above), 113, 114, 115 (above); Keystone, page 25; Mail Newspapers plc, page 38; Mansell Collection, pages 7 (above and below), 55, 95, 101 (left); Mary Evans Picture Library, page 104 (below); Musée Royal de l'Armee, Brussels, page 105 (below); National Portrait Gallery, page 15; New York Times, page 56; Nottingham Evening Post, page 58; Novosti, pages 10, 66 (left), 71; Popperfoto, pages 34 (above and below), 39, 83, 86, 89 (above), 106 (left), 120, 122, 130; *Punch*, pages 6, 73; School of Slavonic and East European Studies, pages 66 (above), 105 (above), 112; Sport and General Press Agency, page 91; Syndication International, page 67; TUC for extract from the *British Worker*, page 59; United States Air Force Art Collection, page 72; Weiner Library, page 116.

The author and publishers are also grateful to the following for permission to reproduce poems:

The estate of Wilfred Owen, the estate of C D Lewis and Chatto & Windus for 'The Sentry', page 115; George Sassoon for 'A Working Party', page 113.

Introduction

OUR LINKS WITH THE PAST

In 1983 the *Sunday Times* carried a report in which a journalist wrote:

> Last Tuesday I shook hands with a man who, when he was two,
> shook hands with a soldier who fought at the battle of Waterloo.
> For a moment I touched history.

Links with the past like this can be experienced every day. You may even know people yourself who lived at the time of the First World War from 1914 to 1918, or who were alive at a time when the Boer War was fought in South Africa and Victoria was Queen.

You can see and touch the past in the buildings and monuments near your home. Churches, castles, abbeys, mansions, houses, mills, paintings and photographs show us what buildings and people looked like in the past. Documents, books and newspapers also tell us what happened in the past. We call this *historical evidence*.

We need to know about the past in order to understand the present. Only if we find out about the early history of European colonialism in Africa can we explain why the policy of apartheid was introduced and why it has isolated South Africa from the rest of the world today. Only if we know something of the history of Ireland can we begin to understand the reasons for the different attitudes taken by people in Northern Ireland and the Irish Republic today.

The Eagle Inn, Ross-on-Wye. It was named after the Lunar Landing Module, Eagle, which was used by Armstrong and Aldrin when they landed on the moon's surface in 1969.

1

With many topics you study in modern world history you may find a local link with the past. The names given to streets, houses, and housing estates, such as John Kennedy Road, Churchill Way, Clem Attlee Court Estate, Mountbatten House, Montgomery Court, Truman House, Victory House, and Kenya Road, recall some of the personalities and important events of the twentieth century. Statues, memorials, inn signs, and house plaques may link your town directly to topics such as the First and Second World Wars, the landings on the moon, or the days of the British Empire.

Checklist — **The Link with the Past**

Go through this checklist when you start a new topic in modern world history.

1   *Find out if there are any features, such as buildings, monuments, street names, or house names near your home which link up in some way with the topic.*

2   *Which of your living relatives (if any) were alive for part of the time covered by the topic? What do they remember about this period?*

3   *What things from the past can you find in your local museum or library which link up with this topic?*

Going through the Checklist

Suppose you are studying the topic of 'The Great War from 1914 to 1918'. This is how you might go through the checklist.

1   *Find out if there are any features, such as buildings, monuments, street names, or house names near your home which link up in some way with the topic.*

You will almost certainly find many war memorials in your home district. Some may depict soldiers in uniform or even carrying weapons. You will probably be able to find out the names of the local regiments and the names of many of the local families who lost several of their members in the fighting. Often the Second World War casualties are recorded on the same memorial. You can then compare the effect of the Second World War on your community with that of the First World War.

2   *Which of your living relatives (if any) were alive for part of the time covered by the topic? What do they remember about this period?*

Your grandparents or great-grandparents may be able to tell you about their experiences of the First World War. Ask them if they remember the soldiers, the work done by women in the War, and whether they can recall Armistice Day on 11 November 1918.

3 *What things from the past can you find in your local museum or library which link up with this topic?*

You may be able to see First World War uniforms, posters, weapons, and photographs in a local museum. You will also find many books in the local library with photographs showing what trench warfare was like at that time.

EXERCISES AND ACTIVITIES

1 *Find out the dates of birth and death of your ancestors. Compile a family tree. See if you can discover what part your ancestors played in the events of the past. Did any of them serve in the armed forces? Did any of them emigrate? Were any of them immigrants from another country?*

2 *Find out which of the museums near your home has exhibits which will help you discover more about the the history of the period you are studying.*

Wedding photograph taken during the First World War

Testing Historical Evidence

WHAT IS HISTORICAL EVIDENCE?

Historians can use only a few of the facts of modern world history. This is why they have to select those facts they think are most important, such as the major wars, peace settlements, and treaties. These are crucial facts because they affect the relations between countries or have an effect on the lives of ordinary people.

In addition, historians also select a few of the many facts which tell us something about the lives and reactions of ordinary people at the time when these important changes were being made. Facts such as these may include a letter from a soldier who fought at Passchendaele, as a volunteer in the Spanish Civil War, or on the Normandy beaches. The letter will help us to picture what it was like to fight in a major battle. It may show us the sacrifices which ordinary people had to make. Yet it will not usually contain crucial facts. Similar examples, chosen from the hundreds of other diaries or letters from soldiers serving at the front, could serve equally well to illustrate the terrors and horrors of modern warfare.

Facts are only facts if they can be proved. We need evidence to show that they are facts and not something which a writer has made up. This means that we need to know the *source* or authority for each fact. Historians divide these historical sources into two main types.

Primary sources always date back to the actual time in the past when the event they record occurred. They are primary sources because they are based on what people saw, or heard, or created at the time. These primary sources may be in the form of words – such as a book, document, or letter. They may be in the form of an illustration, such as a painting, engraving, map, or photograph. They may also be in the shape of a building, an article of clothing, or some other relic you can touch. Some of these different types of primary source are illustrated on these pages.

Secondary sources, by contrast, are almost always in either written or pictorial form. They are usually, but not always, produced at some time (often a long time) after the event or period which they describe or portray. The writer of a secondary source, such as a modern world history book, may use primary sources as well as secondary sources to describe events which happened long ago.

The Daily Telegraph for Friday, 10 September 1976, announcing the death of the great Chinese leader Mao Zedong (or Mao Tse-tung as shown here).

FIGHT FOR POWER AS MAO DIES

Chinese weep in the streets

By NIGEL WADE,
The Daily Telegraph's Peking Correspondent, who is the only British newspaper staff reporter based in China.

CHINA'S 800 million people, a quarter of the world's population, have been instructed to stand to attention for three minutes a week tomorrow in mourning for Chairman Mao Tse-tung, who died yesterday aged 82.

Peking accepted with quiet sorrow the announcement of the death of the god-like symbol of the Chinese Communist revolution.

Two opposing political factions and a group of powerful military commanders must now decide who will lead the nation.

Poster dated 2 December 1919. It can be translated roughly as follows:

GERMAN WORKERS' PARTY
  Munich Branch
      Munich, 2 December 1919

We hereby invite you to a MEETING on Wednesday 10 December 1919, at 7.00 p.m. sharp in the large room of 'The German Empire' Inn, 143 Dachau Street (next to the Number 24 Lori Street Tram Stop).

Speaker: Herr Hitler on 'The Worst Humiliation Facing Germany'

This invitation is a ticket to the meeting. The room is heated.

      The Committee
      Josef Mayer
      Secretary

Deutsche-Arbeiter-Partei
Ortsgruppe München

München, den 2. Dezember 1919

Wir ersuchen Sie hiermit zu der am Mittwoch 10. Dez. 1919
Abends punkt 7 Uhr im grossen Saale des Gasthauses

„ zum Deutschen Reich "

Dachauerstr. 143 (bei Haltestelle Loristr. Linie 24) stattfindenden

Versammlung

bestimmt zu erscheinen
    Redner: Herr H i t l e r über
„ Deutschland vor seiner tiefsten Erniedrigung"
Die Einladung dient als Ausweis. Der Saal ist geheizt.

            Der Ausschuß
            I. A. Josef Mayer
            I. Schriftführer
            Andrästr 10/3 S.B.

THE STATUE OF FREIHEIT?

Cartoon drawn by Bernard Partridge for Punch (6 April 1938) published shortly after Hitler's soldiers had marched into Austria. 'Freiheit' means freedom or liberty. Compare this picture with a view of the real Statue of Liberty in New York.

Signatures of the two German delegates on the Treaty of Versailles, dated 28 June 1919, which brought the First World War to an end.

The Austrian Archduke Ferdinand and his wife leaving the Town Hall shortly before they were assassinated at Sarajevo on 28 June 1914. This was the act which sparked off the outbreak of the First World War.

INSTRUMENT OF ABDICATION

I, Edward the Eighth, of Great Britain, Ireland, and the British Dominions beyond the Seas, King, Emperor of India, do hereby declare My irrevocable determination to renounce the Throne for Myself and for My descendants, and My desire that effect should be given to this Instrument of Abdication immediately.

In token whereof I have hereunto set My hand this tenth day of December, nineteen hundred and thirty six, in the presence of the witnesses whose signatures are subscribed.

SIGNED AT
FORT BELVEDERE
IN THE PRESENCE
OF

The document which Edward VIII signed when giving up (abdicating) the throne in 1936.

In practice, it is sometimes difficult to say whether something is a primary source or a secondary source, unless you are given plenty of information about when, where, why, and how the source was first created. For instance, the sentence – 'The crowd listened in silence; you could have heard a pin drop' – sounds as though it might have been written at the time of the event it is describing. But it could just as easily have been written seventy years later. A picture may look as if it was drawn on the spot but it could have been drawn many years later by an artist in a studio!

Checklist — Historical Evidence

Here are some of the checkpoints you can go through when you see a historical source for the first time.

1 *Can you understand the source? What does it tell you about the past?*

2 *Does it contain abbreviations you have never come across before, references to events or people you do not understand, or words and phrases which we no longer use?*

3 *What type of evidence is it (e.g. a diary entry, a letter, an official report, a book, a cartoon, a photograph)? You can read descriptions of the main types of historical evidence you are most likely to see on pages 46–98.*

4 *Where does the source come from? Can it be trusted? (If you do not know its origin, this does not necessarily mean that the source cannot be trusted. We often get information from newspaper articles and reports written by anonymous writers.)*

5 *When was the source created? Was it created within minutes, hours, days, weeks, months, or years of the event or happening it portrays?*

6 *Is there any statement, or clue, to show that the source is actually based on the writer's own experience or on events which he or she witnessed? In other words, was the writer in a good position to say what happened?*

7 *If the source was written a long time after the event, is there any reason to doubt the accuracy of the facts recalled by the writer?*

8 *Is it a primary or a secondary historical source?*

9 *Was there any particular reason why the source was written? Was it written to please or to annoy anyone? Was it written to justify the writer's actions?*

10 *Are the facts in the source supported by facts you know about from other historical sources?*

Going through the Checklist

Here are two examples of the checklist in action. Notice how checkpoints are ignored if they do not apply to the extract in question.

SOURCE A

On Saturday the 25th Petersburg [later Leningrad] seethed in an atmosphere of extraordinary events from the morning on. The streets, even where there was no concentration of people, were a picture of extreme excitement ... Factories were at a standstill. No trams were running. I don't remember whether any newspapers appeared that day, but in any case events had far outstripped anything the half-stifled press of the day could have conveyed to the people ...

Near the entrance to the 'Letopis' offices, at the gates of the neighbouring factory, I met a small group of civilians, workers by the look of them.

'What do they want?' said one grim-looking fellow. 'They want bread, peace with the Germans, and equality for the Yids.'

'Right in the bull's eye,' I thought, delighted with this brilliant formulation of the programme of the great revolution.

> *The Russian Revolution 1917: A Personal Record by*
> *Nikolai Sukhanov,* translated and edited by
> Joel Carmichael, Oxford 1955

Sukhanov was a socialist friend of Alexander Kerensky, the left-wing Russian leader who was later overthrown by Lenin. Sukhanov's memoirs were originally published in Russian in the Soviet Union in 1922 despite the fact that they were critical of Lenin and the Bolsheviks.

1 *Can you understand the source? What does it tell you about the past?*

It describes events in Petrograd (the name was changed from St Petersburg in 1914) on 25 February 1917 (or 10 March 1917 by our calendar). Over a quarter of a million hungry strikers, exhausted by the war against Germany, had taken to the streets of the city to protest against food shortages. The protests mounted and forced the Czar to abdicate only five days later. In April 1917 Lenin roused the crowds when he gave them the slogan 'PEACE – LAND – BREAD'.

2 *Does it contain abbreviations you have never come across before, references to events or people you do not understand, or words and phrases which we no longer use?*

Yes. 'Yid' is a highly offensive anti-Semitic slang word meaning 'Jew'. 'Formulation' means 'summary'. 'Letopis' was the name of the left-wing magazine to which Sukhanov contributed articles.

3 *What type of evidence is it (e.g. a diary entry, a letter, an official report, a book, a cartoon, a photograph)?*

It is a memoir (see page 63). A memoir is a personal description of events and people as they affected the writer. It is usually written some time afterwards – as opposed to a diary or journal written at the time.

4   *Where does the source come from? Can it be trusted?*

It is written by a left-wing Russian journalist who was an eyewitness in Petrograd at the time and who later took an important part in the 1917 Revolutions. There is no reason to doubt the accuracy of this particular anecdote.

5   *When was the source created?*

About five years after the incident – in 1922.

6   *Is there any statement, or clue, to show that the source is actually based on the writer's own experience or on events which he or she witnessed? Was the writer in a good position to say what happened?*

Yes. He describes his meeting with 'a small group of civilians, workers by the look of them' and records their conversation. As a journalist he was trained to observe and to record the things he saw.

7   *If the source was written a long time after the event is there any reason to doubt the accuracy of the facts recalled by the writer?*

He says 'I don't remember whether any newspapers appeared that day'. If anything, however, this failure to remember an insignificant detail may help to convince us that he could recall accurately the significant details in his story!

Funeral procession for the two hundred victims who died during the March Revolution 1917

8 *Is it a primary or a secondary historical source?*

It is a primary historical source, since it is based on something which the writer witnessed himself only a few years earlier.

9 *Was there any particular reason why the source was written? Was it written to please or to annoy anyone? Was it written to justify the writer's actions?*

Most memoirs are written to justify or explain the writer's actions. They are not objective. Since this particular anecdote closely mirrors the slogan adopted by Lenin — 'PEACE – LAND – BREAD' — we may speculate whether Sukhanov really 'thought' it was 'right in the bull's eye' at the time or whether he did so at a later date when Lenin made it the Bolshevik slogan. What do you think?

10 *Are the facts in the source supported by facts you know about from other historical sources?*

Only the fact that many strikers took to the streets of Petrograd on that day.

The second extract is taken from a newspaper account of the results of the Official Inquiry into the Amritsar Massacre in April 1919.

SOURCE B

General Dyer, giving evidence, said in April last he was in command of the 45th Brigade at Jullundur, and in response to a request for help from Amritsar on April 10 he sent 100 British and 200 Indian soldiers to that city . . .

During the 12th a certain number of arrests were made by the police under military protection. That evening he had a proclamation prepared warning the people against damage to property and violence, and against collecting more than four in number . . .

On the morning of the 13th [April 1919] he decided to go into the city . . . As far as he could remember he reached Jalliamwalla Bagh about 5.15. When he arrived on the scene he proceeded through the narrow entrance on to the high ground and deployed his men on the right and left. Within 30 seconds he ordered fire to be opened. The meeting was then going on and a man was addressing it. At the time of firing he estimated the crowd at 5000, but later on he heard that it was a good deal more . . . His object was to disperse the crowd, and he was going to fire until they were dispersed. The witness added 'In my view the situation at Amritsar was a serious one indeed, and communications I received from the neighbourhood were indicative of a serious rising . . . I looked upon the crowd as rebels, and I considered it was my duty to fire and fire well. There was no other course. I looked upon it as a duty, a very horrible duty.'

The *Daily Telegraph*, 15 December 1919

In fact the Jalliamwalla Bagh was very confined and the crowd had difficulty in escaping through its narrow exits. Dyer did not give them a chance to escape. Instead his soldiers fired 1650 rounds of ammunition into the crowd, killing at least 379 people, and wounding over 1000 others. Six days later he issued an order forcing Indians to crawl along the ground if they wanted to use a street where a lady missionary had been attacked in an earlier incident. These actions were strongly condemned and Dyer was forced to resign from the Army three months later.

1   *Can you understand the source? What does it tell you about the past?*

It describes the Amritsar Massacre of 1919 from the point of view of the general responsible for killing nearly 400 civilians.

2   *Does it contain abbreviations you have never come across before, references to events or people you do not understand, or words and phrases which we no longer use?*

The Jalliamwalla Bagh was an open space in the city centre.

3   *What type of evidence is it (e.g. a diary entry, a letter, an official report, a book, a cartoon, a photograph)?*

It is a newspaper report quoting evidence given to an Official Inquiry.

4   *Where does the source come from? Can it be trusted?*

Since the journalist is describing the evidence heard by the Official Inquiry (a type of law court investigating the reasons for the massacre) we can be fairly certain that this is an accurate report of what General Dyer actually said to the Tribunal. But, obviously, it is *not necessarily* an accurate report of what actually happened on the day of the massacre. That was why the Official Inquiry was being held.

5   *When was the source created?*

Some time before 15 December 1919.

6   *Is there any statement, or clue, to show that the source is actually based on the writer's own experience or on events which he or she witnessed? Was the writer in a good position to say what happened?*

It is a direct report of the evidence given by General Dyer. The general, of course, was in the best position of all to say what happened at Amritsar. But since he was under investigation for his actions he is not necessarily a reliable witness.

7   *If the source was written a long time after the event, is there any reason to doubt the accuracy of the facts recalled by the writer?*

General Dyer was recalling events which occurred only eight months earlier, yet he was described as having said, '*As far as he could remember* he reached Jalliamwalla Bagh about 5.15'. You might have expected an experienced army officer to know *exactly* when he reached the scene of the place where 379 people were killed within minutes of his arrival.

8 *Is it a primary or a secondary historical source?*

It is a primary historical source, since it describes at first hand an incident which occurred only eight months earlier.

9 *Was there any particular reason why the source was written? Was it written to please or to annoy anyone? Was it written to justify the writer's actions?*

Obviously General Dyer's army career was at stake. His evidence could only be directed towards clearing his name.

10 *Are the facts in the source supported by facts you know about from other historical sources?*

Yes. General Dyer did not dispute the fact that he fired on the crowd. What was at issue was why he did it and whether or not his actions were justified.

British troops in India in the 1920s

EXERCISES AND ACTIVITIES

1 *Use the checklist printed on page 8 to check through Source A below. Can you tell whether the writer was an eyewitness to this event or not?*

SOURCE A

In the presence of an enormous crowd of about 100 000 people lining the road for a distance of four miles [6.4 km], amid a swelling chorus of 'Long Live Gandhi!'.... Mr. Gandhi set out this morning to open the campaign for Independence ...

Wealthy Hindus and impoverished labourers vied in hailing the Mahatma and as the procession slowly moved along, the crowds showered upon him coins, currency notes, flowers and saffron ...

Daily News & Chronicle, 13 March 1930

The author of Source B (below) was an 18-year-old Londoner. On Saturday, 7 September 1940 he cycled into the countryside south of London.

SOURCE B

Weekend: 7–8 September
Pandemonium broke loose right above me. I jumped off my bike and looked up. It was the most amazing, impressive, riveting sight. Directly above me were literally hundreds of 'planes, Germans! The sky was full of them. Bombers hemmed in with fighters, like bees around their queen, like destroyers round the battleship, so came Jerry. My ears were deafened by bombs, machine-gun fire, the colossal inferno of machine after machine zooming in the blue sky . . . Looking up – squadron after squadron of Spitfires and Hurricanes tore out of the blue, one by one they tore the Nazi formations into shreds. 'Planes scattered left and right, and the terrible battle came lower.

Colin Perry, *Boy in the Blitz,* Leo Cooper, 1972

2   *Look at Source B and go through the checklist on page 8.*

What famous battle was the author describing?

HAS THE EVIDENCE BEEN ALTERED?

Most of the historical evidence that you will see will probably have been altered in some way.

Almost all the extracts you read will form only a very small part of a much bigger whole, such as a small paragraph taken from a newspaper of thirty-two pages, or a few sentences from a 600-page book.

Sometimes the text of the extract may have been altered to make it easier for you to read. Extra punctuation may have been added. Old spellings may have been corrected. Words we no longer use may have had their nearest modern meanings inserted into the extract – often inside square brackets to set them apart from ordinary curved brackets.

In many cases large parts of an extract will have been left out simply because there is not enough space to include the whole of the extract in a book, on an examination paper, or in a collection of historical documents. Often the intervening words and sentences are left out because they are difficult to understand today, irrelevant, or just boring! Missing text is sometimes shown by a row of dots like this: . . . This is called an ellipsis (or ellipses if more than one). It is usually impossible to tell whether the dots show that just one or two words are missing or whether they indicate that several pages have been left out. In many extracts the ellipses will not be shown, since their inclusion every time a word, phrase, sentence, or paragraph is omitted would make the text unreadable.

Omitting words, phrases, sentences, or even punctuation marks can alter the meaning of an extract.

EXERCISES AND ACTIVITIES

Many important documents and historical records have been destroyed by accident (such as in a fire) or by people who were ignorant of (or could not have known of, or suspected) their later importance (such as the childhood diaries of a future world leader). Undoubtedly some documents have been destroyed in order to conceal the truth. Only rarely do we have actual proof of this. Here is an example, taken from the diary of Frances Stevenson, the secretary and mistress of David Lloyd George. He was the British prime minister during the First World War and had been involved in a row with General Maurice in 1918. The general claimed that Lloyd George misled the House of Commons by quoting inaccurate statistics about the number of troops fighting on the Western Front. Lloyd George successfully denied this in Parliament. Frances Stevenson recalled these events when she wrote this entry in her diary sixteen years later, at a time when she was helping Lloyd George to write his memoirs of the First World War.

Frances Stevenson

October 5th 1934
Have been reading up the events connected with the Maurice Debate in order to help D. [David Lloyd George] with this Chapter in Vol. V, and am uneasy in my mind about an incident which occurred at the time & which is known only to J.T. Davies & myself. D. obtained from the W.O. [War Office] the figures which he used in his statement on April 9th in the House of Commons on the subject of manpower. These figures were afterwards stated by Gen. Maurice to be inaccurate. I was in J.T. Davies' room a few days after the statement, & J.T. was sorting out red dispatch boxes to be returned to the Departments. As was his wont, he looked in them before locking them up & sending them out to the

Messengers. Pulling out a W.O. box he found in it, to his great astonishment, a paper from the D.M.O. [Department of Military Operations] containing modifications & corrections of the first figures they had sent, & by some mischance this box had remained unopened. J.T. & I examined it in dismay, & then J.T. put it in the fire, remarking, 'Only you and I, Frances, know of the existence of this paper.'

Frances Stevenson, *Lloyd George: A Diary*, edited by
A.J.P. Taylor, Hutchinson 1971

1   *Go through the checklist on page 8.*

2   *Who were J.T., and D., and what were the D.M.O., and the W.O.?*

3   *Why did J.T. put the document in the fire?*

4   *Why was J.T. incorrect in saying 'Only you and I, Frances, know of the existence of this paper'. Who else must have known that it existed?*

5   *How likely do you think it is that Frances Stevenson would have been able to recall J.T.'s exact remarks over sixteen years after they were made?*

6   *How is this incident a warning to historians?*

David Lloyd George

FACT OR OPINION?

We need no proof of some of the facts of modern world history because we can see the events for ourselves on live television. Such an event was the treaty on reducing nuclear weapons which was signed by the American President, Ronald Reagan, and the Soviet leader, Mikhail Gorbachev, in front of hundreds of millions of television viewers throughout the world in December 1987. But facts like this, which we can witness for ourselves, are very few in comparison with those we have to take on trust from other sources.

Events in the past are historical facts because historians have evidence to prove that the events actually happened. Historians always need proof. In many ways they are like lawyers in a law court. They obtain evidence from witnesses. They examine exhibits. They argue. They reach a conclusion or verdict. In a court of law, the judge and the jury try to decide the case on the basis of the facts, not the opinions. So, too, do historians. When the members of a jury reach a decision on the basis of those facts they express an opinion themselves. Most times they are probably right. Sometimes they are wrong. So it is, too, with historians.

Sometimes it is difficult to tell if a statement is fact or opinion. If you know little about the subject you will probably have to accept the statement as fact for the moment unless it is clear that it could never be proved or disproved to everyone's satisfaction. Statements of fact are often misleading because they are not precise enough or because they contain insufficient details. For instance, if you read the following statement quickly – *'Germans worried by unemployment welcomed Hitler with open arms'* – you may accept it as a statement of fact because you do know that:

(a) many Germans were worried by the appalling problem of unemployment during the Depression years of the 1930s;
(b) many Germans voted for Hitler and the National Socialist Party in the elections of the early 1930s.

But you also know that many Germans – journalists, professors, Jews, Communists, Socialists, trade-unionists, the clergy, intellectuals, artists, etc., – were strongly opposed to Hitler. Were they *not* worried by unemployment as well?

The statement would make more sense if it was reworded – *'The Germans who welcomed Hitler with open arms were worried by unemployment'* – but even this cannot be accepted as fact. It is still an opinion, since we have no way of knowing for certain that unemployment was the key issue with the Germans who voted for Hitler. Nor can we be certain what is meant by 'welcomed Hitler with open arms'. This will mean different things to different people. Voting for Hitler at an election did not make a German a wholehearted supporter of the Nazi Party. The statement needs to be qualified. We could probably accept it as fact, if it read like this – *'Many of the Germans who voted for Hitler were worried by unemployment'*.

Checklist — **Facts and Opinions**

Use your common sense if you are asked to say whether you think part of an extract is an opinion rather than a fact. Ask yourself:

1 *Which parts of the statement can probably be proved right or wrong? A specific statement, such as the name of a person or place, a date, number, or quantity, is something which can be proved, or disproved, as a fact. Either the name, place, date, number, or quantity is correct or it is not. The same thing applies to specific events or happenings which can also be easily proved or disproved. Either they did happen or they did not. This is a question of fact and not of opinion.*

2 *Which parts of the statement are obviously opinions and not facts? You can often detect opinions where the writer uses words which have no precise meaning, such as* popular, beautiful, deeply, friendly, unpleasant, ugly, *and* unwise. *By contrast many words, such as* French-speaking, blue, fifty, *and* baker, *have factual meanings.*

Bear in mind that opinions are often very useful to a historian because they show what people felt about an issue, or an event in the past. But beware of thinking that opinions are facts simply because you agree with them!

Going through the Checklist

The following extract is from the private diary kept by Dr Josef Goebbels, Nazi Minister for Propaganda. He was preparing to broadcast Hitler's proclamation to the German people announcing the start of Operation Barbarossa – the German invasion of the Soviet Union. As Minister for Propaganda, Goebbels was used to distorting the truth in order to get the backing of the German people for Nazi policies.

22 June 1941 (Sunday)

The attack will begin at 3.30 a.m. 160 Full Divisions along a 3000 kilometre-long battlefront. Everything is well prepared. The biggest concentration of forces in the history of the world. The Führer seems to lose his fear as the decision comes nearer. It is always the same with him. He relaxes visibly. All the exhaustion seems to drop away. We pace up and down in his salon for three hours . . .

    I go over to the ministry. It is still pitch dark. I put my colleagues in the picture. Total amazement in all quarters. Most had guessed half, or even the whole truth. Everyone sets to work immediately.

Radio, press and newsreel are mobilised. Everything runs like clockwork . . . 3.30. Now the guns will be thundering. May God bless our weapons!

Outside on the Wilhelmplatz, it is quiet and deserted. Berlin and the entire Reich are asleep. I have half an hour to spare, but I cannot sleep. I pace up and down restlessly in my room. One can hear the breath of history.'

The Goebbels Diaries 1939–1941,
translated and edited by Fred Taylor,
Hamish Hamilton, 1982

1 *Which parts of the statement can probably be proved right or wrong?*

Some elements of this statement, such as the pacing up and down, the quietness on the Wilhelmplatz, etc., may be fact or fiction – it is of no importance. The crucial facts are the time of the attack (at 3.30 a.m.), the size of the German Army (160 Divisions) and the length of the battlefront (3000 km). These are facts which can be easily proved right or wrong. Nor need we doubt that it was, indeed, the biggest concentration of forces in the history of the world. Of lesser importance is his factual description of his actions at the Ministry in telling his colleagues the news of the impending invasion and their obvious response – to get down to work immediately to prepare radio, press and newsreel coverage.

2 *Which parts of the statement are obviously opinions and not facts?*

Since Goebbels was the Minister responsible, his statements that 'everything is well prepared' and 'everything ran like clockwork' are obviously opinions and not facts. His descriptions of Hitler's reactions as the crucial hour approached are also opinions – as is the description of the amazement of his colleagues when he told them the news of the impending invasion of the Soviet Union.

Dr Josef Goebbels

EXERCISES AND ACTIVITIES

Crowds attending the funeral of Lenin in 1924

Read through the following extracts from accounts which appeared in two British newspapers on 23 January 1924, two days after the death of Lenin (real name Vladimir Ilyitch Oulianoff), the 'Architect of the Russian Revolution'.

SOURCE A

The great leader of Bolshevism is dead . . . Lenin vanishes from the vast turmoil he has created.

Russia, resurrected from her ruins, will sit one day in judgement on his memory. For us it suffices to say that, with Lenin dead, a figure of Satanic proportions has departed from the European arena.

I well remember, and am not likely to forget, the sinister impression produced upon me by Lenin when I met him face-to-face in 1918 at the very beginning of his dictatorship . . . Although he smiled nearly all the time there was something 'macabre' in his appearance. The bloodthirsty Commissars of the Extraordinary Commission, with whom I played a dangerous game of hide-and-seek for many long months, had never been able to put the cold hand of terror round my heart as this small, shabbily dressed, uncouth looking man was able to do from the first minute he entered the room where the conference was taking place . . .

I thought to myself that surely this man, who was not afraid to dominate the [working classes] would go far on the road to a complete dictatorship of Russia. And so it happened.

The *Daily Telegraph,* 23 January 1924

SOURCE B

Lenin is dead.

Through all Russia that news has struck as the news of a deep and personal loss. For 'Ilyitch' was loved of his own Russian people – whom he understood and loved so well – as no leader of men in our time has been loved . . .

Under his dominant leadership, the Bolsheviks, because they were clearminded and resolute, took Russia from the nerveless grasp of Kerensky and his fellows . . . and started to build on the ruins of the old order the first Socialist Republic of the World . . .

His fearless honesty, his outspoken truthsaying when truthsaying was hard and unpopular; his absolute integrity; the simplicity of his private life; his deep sympathies; his mischievous sense of humour – all these won him the love of all who worked with him.

Incomparably – agree or disagree with his policies, his methods, his views – he stands out in history as the greatest spokesman, the greatest leader that the working-class movement has yet known, as one of the greatest leaders the world has known.

W.N.E. in the *Daily Herald,* 23 January 1924

1 *Use the checklist on historical evidence printed on page 8 to test each of these two sources in turn.*

2 *Which parts of Source A and Source B can probably be proved right or wrong?*

3 *Which parts of Source A and Source B are obviously opinions and not facts?*

4 *How does the account in the* Daily Telegraph *compare with the one printed in the* Daily Herald? *How are they similar? How do they differ from each other? How do you account for these differences?*

5 *Write your own newspaper account of the death of Lenin. Phrase it in such a way that it might have been equally acceptable as a news item in both the* Daily Telegraph *and the* Daily Herald *on 23 January 1924.*

ACCURACY AND RELIABILITY

Most of the extracts which you will see will be far too short for you ever to say with confidence that they are trustworthy and reliable sources of information. On the other hand you may be able to detect mistakes or inaccuracies in an extract which throw some doubt on the reliability of the historical source from which the extract is taken.

Checklist — **Accuracy and Reliability**

Ask yourself these questions.

1 *Are there any obvious mistakes or errors of fact in the extract? We can often test for mistakes by comparing one historical source with another. If there are mistakes it does not necessarily mean that the rest of the source is inaccurate. Nor does it mean that the source has no value. But it does mean that you should exercise some caution in treating the rest of the source as a reliable source of information.*

2 *Have you any reason to think that the facts quoted in the account may give an exaggerated or distorted view of the events which actually occurred?*

3 *Has the author left out any obvious facts which tell a different story from the one conveyed by the extract? Is there any reason to think that they were left out deliberately? (It may be that the author was just unaware or ignorant of these facts or could not have known about them anyway.)*

4 *Has the author used any words or phrases which show that he or she approves or disapproves of a person, an action, or an event? Does the author show any signs of being biased or prejudiced (see pages 26–32)?*

Going through the Checklist

Source A which follows is an extract from a biography of Lloyd George, first published in 1954. We can test the accuracy and reliability of this statement about the suffragettes by comparing the facts in this extract with those in newspapers published in June 1913 at the time of the incident which it describes (Sources B to F).

SOURCE A

SUFFRAGETTES

The most determined martyr of them all, Miss Emily Davidson, red-haired, green-eyed, half-demented girl, denied the sacrifice of her life when she leapt from an upper floor in Holloway Prison after a hunger-strike, was killed in the end on Derby Day, 1913, when she flung herself under the flying hooves of the King's horse as it led the field, thundering round Tattenham Corner.

Frank Owen, Tempestuous Journey: Lloyd George
His Life and Times, Hutchinson, 1954

SOURCE B

ABOYEUR'S DERBY

At Tattenham Corner, and after rounding it, he [Aboyeur] still maintained his place [as leader of the field].

The Times, Thursday, 5 June 1913

SOURCE C

NARRATIVES OF SPECTATORS

The general impression of those who saw the incident at close quarters seemed to be that the woman had seized hold of the first horse she could reach – which happened to be the King's – not with the intention of disqualifying any particular horse, but of interfering with and, if possible, spoiling the race as a whole.

The Times, Thursday, 5 June 1913

SOURCE D

AN EYEWITNESS

They had just got round the Corner and all had passed but the King's horse, when a woman squeezed through the railings and ran out into the course. She made straight for Anmer, and made a sort of leap for the reins. I think she got hold of them, but it was impossible to say.

An eyewitness account in the *Manchester Guardian,*
Thursday, 5 June 1913

SOURCE E

DEATH OF MISS DAVISON

Miss Emily Wilding Davison, the suffragist who interfered with the King's horse during the race for the Derby, died in hospital at Epsom at 4.50 yesterday afternoon.

The Times, Monday, 9 June 1913

SOURCE F

INQUEST ON EMILY WILDING DAVISON
[Tuesday, 10 June 1913]

Police-sergeant Bunn said he was about twenty yards [18 metres] away from Miss Davison when she rushed out on the course. 'I saw the woman throw her hands up in front of the horses. Some had previously passed her.'

The Coroner, in summing up, said he did not think that Miss Davison aimed at the King's horse in particular but that her intention was to upset the race. The jury would probably dismiss from their minds the idea that she intended to take her life.

The jury returned a verdict of 'Death by misadventure'.

The Suffragette, Friday, 13 June 1913

SOURCE G

*Tombstone at Morpeth,
Northumberland*

1 *Are there any obvious mistakes or errors of fact in the extract (i.e. Source A)?*

Yes.
(a) The tombstone (Source G) shows clearly that her surname was Davison not Davidson.
(b) She died in hospital on Sunday, 8 June not on Derby Day itself – Wednesday, 4 June (Sources E and G).
(c) The King's horse (Anmer) did not lead the field at Tattenham Corner. The eventual winner, a horse called Aboyeur, was the leader (Source B).

2 *Have you any reason to think that the facts in the account may give a distorted view of the events which actually occurred?*

Yes. There is no evidence that 'she flung herself under the flying hooves of the King's horse'. Quite the contrary.
(a) Two of the sources (C and F) indicated that it was sheer accident that she was knocked down by the King's horse. In other words, she did not specifically select the King's horse in order to make her protest.
(b) Far from flinging herself *under* the horse, one eyewitness (Source D) said she made 'a sort of leap for the reins' and this was confirmed by a police officer at the inquest (Source F).

3 *Has the author left out any obvious facts which tell a different story from the one conveyed by the extract?*

Yes. The author describes her as 'The most determined martyr of them all' but fails to say that the inquest jury returned a verdict of 'Death by misadventure' (Source F).

4 *Has the author used any words or phrases which show that he or she approves or disapproves of a person, an action, or an event? Does the author show any signs of being biased or prejudiced (see pages 26–32)?*

Yes. The use of the phrase 'half-demented' is intended to suggest that Emily Davison was halfway towards being insane. This was not the verdict of the jury at the inquest (Source F). The use of adjectives such as 'red-haired' and 'green-eyed' can also be interpreted as indicating bias, since they are obviously intended to suggest that she was unbalanced, wilful, headstrong and envious of others. Nor was she a 'girl' (with its implication of inexperience and impetuousness). As you can see from her tombstone (Source G), she was a mature woman of 40 years of age.

EXERCISES AND ACTIVITIES

1 *Compare Source H (below) with Sources I, J, and K which follow.*

2 *Use the checklist on historical evidence on page 8 to examine each source first of all.*

3 *Then use the checklist on page 22 to identify any possible inaccuracies or inconsistencies in these extracts.*

On Sunday, 3 September 1939, Hitler's interpreter, Dr Paul Schmidt, took Ribbentrop's place at the German Foreign Office in Berlin to receive the ultimatum from the British ambassador, Sir Nevile Henderson, giving Germany just two hours to agree to withdraw German troops from Poland.

SOURCE H

I then took the ultimatum to the Chancellery, where everyone was anxiously awaiting me ... When I entered the next room Hitler was sitting at his desk and Ribbentrop stood by the window. Both looked up expectantly as I came in. I stopped at some distance from Hitler's desk, and then slowly translated the British Government's ultimatum. When I finished there was complete silence.

Hitler sat immobile, gazing before him. He was not at a loss, as was afterwards stated, nor did he rage as others allege. He sat completely silent and unmoving.

After an interval which seemed an age, he turned to Ribbentrop, who had remained standing by the window. 'What now?' asked Hitler with a savage look, as though implying that his Foreign Minister had misled him about England's probable reaction.

Paul Schmidt, *Hitler's Interpreter*,
edited by R.H.C. Steed, Heinemann, 1951

Hitler with Ribbentrop

SOURCE I

BERLIN
3 September

At nine o'clock this morning Sir Nevile Henderson called on the German Foreign Minister and handed him a note giving Germany until eleven o'clock to accept the British demand that Germany withdraw her troops from Poland.

William L. Shirer, *Berlin Diary,* Hamish Hamilton, 1941

SOURCE J

RIBBENTROP GIVES REPLY TO BRITISH ENVOY

Berlin, Sunday, Sept. 3 (AP) – German Foreign Minister Joachim von Ribbentrop received British Ambassador Sir Nevile Henderson at 9 a.m. today to hand him Germany's answer to the 'final warnings' of Britain and France.

The New York Times, Sunday, 3 September 1939

SOURCE K

The British declaration of war, however, took him [Hitler] by surprise. Dr Paul Schmidt, his interpreter, recorded his reaction. 'Hitler was petrified and utterly disconcerted. After a while he turned to Ribbentrop and asked "What now?".'

Brigadier Peter Young, *Wars of the 20th Century,*
Bison Books, 1985

BIAS AND PREJUDICE

Bias in history presents one side of the picture only, such as setting out only those arguments you agree with, or listing only the good or bad points (but not both). It may exaggerate or distort what someone has done or said.

An advertisement is an obvious example of bias. It does not tell you the bad points about a product. Nor does it tell you about better products from other manufacturers!

Similar bias can be found in both primary and secondary historical sources. People often gloss over, or ignore, bad points and the other side of an argument. They may select only those facts which support their case. They may use words designed to make readers feel strongly either for or against a particular point of view. Bias is often political or religious.

A historian must study evidence carefully to see if it is biased in any way. If there is bias, it does not mean the source is valueless. Far from it. The source may be valuable precisely because it reveals the attitudes of a large group of people. It shows how people felt and thought at the time.

Prejudice is an extreme form of bias. Prejudice does not listen to reason. Prejudice can be suspected if a writer is known to have, or reveals, a hatred, dislike, or an unreasonable attitude to particular people or places. This can sometimes happen, even in the writings of well-known historians. Political or religious beliefs, for instance, can sometimes lead to a very biased selection of evidence and lead the writer to a faulty conclusion. Prejudice can often be seen in writings about:

- a particular race of people (e.g. the Arabs or the Jews),
- a person – particularly one with controversial opinions, such as Karl Marx, the founder of modern communism
- the part played by women in society or in politics
- a political party (e.g. Communist, Socialist, Conservative)
- a class of people (e.g. upper, middle, or working class)
- a minority group
- a religion
- a way of life (e.g. that of the gypsies).

Anti-Semitic Nazi propaganda from 1937. How did this poster encourage the German people to be prejudiced against Jews? What does it tell us about the Nazis?

Bias and prejudice can be expressed in pictures as well, such as in pictures which caricature ethnic groups and foreigners.

You may be able to understand, or even appreciate, why there is bias – such as the bias in favour of Napoleon by a French historian and the bias in favour of Nelson or Wellington by a British historian. Nonetheless, it is still bias.

If you see or suspect bias in a historical extract you should treat the whole of the extract with caution. The writer may have allowed bias to alter the way in which certain facts are chosen and other facts left out.

When we read a newspaper, we do not often find concrete evidence that this has happened. In the following extract, however, you can see how the powerful owner of a newspaper, Lord Northcliffe ('the Chief'), tried to win support for David Lloyd George in the *Daily Mail* on 6 December 1916, at the height of the First World War. Lloyd George had just resigned from Asquith's Cabinet because he felt the war was not being fought vigorously enough.

> Wednesday, December 6, 1916: Things came to a head last night and Asquith resigned. And our shout to-day across the splash page is, 'BRAVO! LLOYD GEORGE.' The King sent for Bonar Law last night. Our private information is that Lloyd George is willing to serve under anybody who is out to win the war, and that Bonar Law is his nominee for the leadership of the new Ministry. We print to-day pictures of Lloyd George and Asquith side by side. 'Get a smiling picture of Lloyd George,' said the Chief, 'and underneath it put the caption "DO IT NOW," and get the worst possible picture of Asquith and label it "WAIT AND SEE".'
>
> He asked me what I thought of this: 'It's rather – unkind, to say the least, isn't it?' I said. 'Nothing of the sort,' he said. 'Rough methods are needed if we are not to lose this war ... it's the only way. This Haldane gang has dragged the country into a dangerous mess.'
>
> Other inspired headings to-day are: 'Germans Fear Lloyd George: France Wants Him: The Empire Trusts Him.'

Tom Clarke, *My Northcliffe Diary,* Victor Gollancz, 1931

BRAVO, LLOYD GEORGE!

MR. ASQUITH RESIGNS.

A TORN-UP AGREEMENT.

THE KING SENDS FOR MR. BONAR LAW.

MR. LLOYD GEORGE GETS HIS WAR COUNCIL.

COURT CIRCULAR.

BUCKINGHAM PALACE, Tuesday.

The Right Hon. H. H. Asquith had an audience of his Majesty this evening and tendered his resignation as Prime Minister and First Lord of the Treasury, which the King was graciously pleased to accept.

Mr. Asquith was received in audience by his Majesty at Buckingham Palace shortly before seven o'clock, when he tendered his resignation.

Mr. Bonar Law arrived at Buckingham Palace shortly after 9.30 in response to a summons from his Majesty. He left again at 10.10.

Mr. Bonar Law owes his position entirely to Mr. Lloyd George's action. The position of Mr. Lloyd George amid the events of yesterday and last night remains the same. He stands for a "War-Forward Movement" and is willing to serve under anybody who is "out to win the war."

Mr. Lloyd George feels that no personal considerations on his or [...] tion was prompted by strong representations from his personal supporters in the Cabinet. In particular the following are stated to have persuaded Mr. Asquith to tear up the agreement of Monday:—

Viscount Grey,	Mr. Harcourt.
Mr. Runciman.	Lord Crewe.
Mr. McKenna.	

In such circumstances Mr. Lloyd George could but offer his resignation, and he did so in writing.

Mr. Lloyd George made no overtures. He was determined not to budge an inch from the only plan, in his opinion, that will wage war successfully.

Then it was, in the language of the Hide-the-Truth Press, that Mr. Asquith "put his foot down," and [...]

Prime Minister. The general opinion of our people is that they do not think the crisis ought to have arisen. The Labour Party are quite prepared to see a speeding-up of the war and are also prepared to accept a smaller War Council, but they do not think it should be arrived at by the means which have been adopted. They recognise the great driving force of Mr. Lloyd George, but they feel in a crisis of this kind the proposal to overthrow the Prime Minister is not a proper policy or one to be supported.

There is good reason to doubt whether this statement represents the opinion of the Labour Party, which consists of 35 members. The Simonites consist of a number of M.P.s who represent nobody in particular, unless the conscientious objector is to be counted as somebody.

How little the Hide-the-Truth Press understood the crisis is shown by the announcement in yesterday's *Westminster Gazette,* which prided itself on being the organ through which reports of [...]

DO IT NOW.

WHAT MR. LLOYD GEORGE HAS DONE IN WAR.

Mr. Lloyd George's work during the war has two commanding qualities. The first is that he grasped the importance of time; he acted swiftly with the least possible delay. The second is that he understood the magnitude of the conflict and the stupendous difficulty of the task. While others dealt in words he was studying realities. *He was indeed a force in the Government like the spring that drives the watch.*

On the outbreak of war he was Chancellor of the Exchequer. He was confronted with unparalleled difficulties when Great Britain declared war on August 4, 1914. *The foreign exchanges had collapsed. Credit was tottering. Prices on the Stock Exchange were falling with terrific speed. Gold was being swept out of the country.*

He acted with amazing energy and decision. A moratorium was enforced to [...]

DO IT NOW!

WAIT AND SEE!

nice credit a breathing-time. A guarantee was given by the State for certain liabilities. The banking machinery [...]

GERMANS FEAR MR. LLOYD GEORGE.

FRANCE WANTS HIM.

THE EMPIRE TRUSTS HIM.

Comment from Berlin, Paris, the Over-seas Dominions, and New York on Mr. Lloyd George's position in the Cabinet crisis can be summed up as follows:—

1. The Germans fear him as the one man who means more active war upon them and prevents them from obtaining an honourable peace—i.e., a peace that will suit Germany.

2. The Allies like him as the man of action instead of words.

3. The Empire trusts him for the same reason.

4. The United States says of him : "He was right just as often as the others were wrong."

'RELENTLESS ANTI-GERMAN'

HUN REJOICING AT MR. LLOYD GEORGE'S "FALL."

BERNE, Tuesday.

The German Press expresses the keenest satisfaction at Mr. Lloyd George's rumoured resignation. It regards his retirement as the downfall of the most relentless anti-German among the Allies.

The *Baierischer Kurier* says : "This is a terrible disaster for the war party in England."

The *Leipziger Tageblatt* says:" The British people have doubtless had enough of this war agitator. His fall from power brings nearer an honourable peace for Germany."

—Wireless Press.

From Our Special Correspondent.

AMSTERDAM, Tuesday. [...]

ter of referendum. He considers that an assembly, however sympathetic, of twenty-three Ministers cannot reply with sufficient rapidity to the decision of a single Hindenburg, and still less anticipate him.

In time of war the answering thrust must be immediate and the initiative instantaneous. If Mr. Lloyd George has his way Sir Edward Carson, with his brilliant qualities, will co-operate in the Ministry, and his immense naval and military war Great Britain is waging in Europe, Asia, and Africa will be effectively directed by three or four energetic, clear-headed men who can meet and come to decisions at any hour of the day or night.

We French can only wish complete success to the new Ministerial organisation. Our people, who are perfectly conscious of the utility of swift and strong management of affairs, will applaud all the initiative taken by the Entente in reply to the latest and offensious dispositions of our enemies.

THE GREEK WARNING.

M. Stephen Pichon in the *Petit Journal* declares:—

It is evidently not to weaken Britain's defences and diminish the power of her defensive that Mr. Lloyd George has acted. It is to emphasise the urgency of more energetic and better co-ordinated military, industrial, political, and diplomatic action. It is to render possible the remedying of a situation which, in his opinion, leaves much to be desired, since its distinguishing signs are the events in Roumania, the Greek rising, the unsatisfactory results on the eastern front, and the incardescence of naval warfare which the British Admiralty has been unable to prevent.

The *Gaulois,* commenting upon the "salutary crisis" provoked by Mr. Lloyd George's action, remarks:

He has grasped, as no one in this country has grasped, how indispensable it is in the second of our military effort to extract the conduct of the war to men of determination and competence. He has thus reached a solution of the problem that seemed to [...]

The Daily Mail, 6 December 1916

Checklist — **Bias and Prejudice**

Study the source carefully. If possible, compare the facts in the extract with other evidence, including engravings and photographs.

1 *Which words, phrases, and sentences seem to you to be opinions rather than facts (see pages 17–21)?*

2 *Are these opinions based on all the facts or only on certain facts which support the opinion in question?*

3 *Does anything in the extract contradict facts which you already know to be true?*

4 *Does the writer appear to take sides by presenting only one side of an argument or by showing only one side in a favourable or unfavourable light?*

5 *Is any part of the extract an obvious lie or exaggeration?*

6 *Has the writer used colourful words or phrases to try to influence the way you feel about the facts? For instance, an action may be described as being 'brave' or 'courageous' in one writer's view and 'foolhardy' or 'irresponsible' in an opposing view.*

7 *Are any of the statements controversial? This means anything with which some other people are almost certain to disagree.*

Going through the Checklist

The following extracts are taken from accounts of the show trials and purges which took place in the Soviet Union between 1936 and 1938. Thousands of senior members of the ruling Communist Party were put on trial and most were sentenced to death. They included all the members of Lenin's old Politburo (apart from Stalin), such as Zinoviev, Kamenev and Bukharin, the Red Army Chief, Marshal Tukhachevsky, and the Navy Chief, Admiral Orlov. Trotsky, the arch-enemy of Stalin, was already in exile but was hunted down and assassinated by Stalin's agents in Mexico in 1940. When the purges came to an end it was estimated that at least one million Russians had been executed and a further eight million sent to labour camps in Siberia.

SOURCE A

... in the late spring of 1936, a series of arrests of Nazi agents and Trotskyist conspirators revealed the existence of a much wider organisation – a central terrorist committee which included, not only Zinoviev and Kamenev, but several leading Trotskyists. Preliminary investigations and evidence given at their trial (in August 1936) revealed that ... the organisation was in close contact with the German Gestapo. Zinoviev, Kamenev and their associates were sentenced to be shot ...

Abroad, these trials aroused volumes of speculation, invention and abuse: abuse so sharp, indeed, that it was commonly regarded among ordinary Soviet citizens, as those who met them in these years could testify, as the most convincing proof that the Soviet Government had really struck a crushing blow at plans which had been hatched outside its borders, and that those who were responsible for the hatching were squealing.

Andrew Rothstein, *A History of the U.S.S.R.,* Penguin 1950

After Stalin died in 1953, the new First Secretary of the Communist Party, Nikita Khruschev, helped to set up a Commission to look into the purges of the 1930s. Khruschev surprised the world when he made a famous speech at a secret session of the Twentieth Party Congress in 1956.

SOURCE B

The Commission has become acquainted with a large quantity of materials in the N.K.V.D. [Secret Police] archives and with other documents and has established many facts pertaining to the fabrication of cases against Communists, to false accusations, to glaring abuses of Soviet legality – which resulted in the death of innocent people. It became apparent that many Party, Soviet and economic activists who were branded in 1937–38 as 'enemies' were actually never enemies, spies, wreckers, etc., but were always honest Communists; they were only so stigmatized and often, no longer able to bear barbaric tortures, they charged themselves (at the order of the investigative judges – falsifiers) with all kinds of grave and unlikely crimes.

Khruschev Remembers, translated by Strobe Talbott, Andre Deutsch 1971

SOURCE C

Show trial in the Soviet Union in the 1930s. The accused men are sitting on the right between the armed guards. A Soviet radio broadcast at about that time announced that 'The Trotsky–Fascist criminals who have made an attempt against the property of the Soviet State . . . have deserved their merciless punishment. This is the sentence of our great country – Death to the Enemies of the People.'

SOURCE D

Later investigation established the fact that these villains [Zinoviev, Kamenev, etc.] had been engaged in espionage and in organizing acts of diversion. The full extent of the monstrous moral and political depravity of these men, their despicable villainy and treachery, concealed by hypocritical professions of loyalty to the Party, were revealed at a trial held in Moscow in 1936.

The chief instigator and ringleader of this gang of assassins and spies was Judas Trotsky. . . .

[The 1937 trials] brought to light the fact that the Trotsky-Bukharin fiends, in obedience to the wishes of their masters - the espionage services of foreign states - had set out to destroy the Party and the Soviet state . . .

These Whiteguard pigmies, whose strength was no more than that of a gnat, apparently flattered themselves that they were the masters of the country. . . .

These Whiteguard insects forgot that the real masters of the Soviet country were the Soviet people . . .

These contemptible lackeys of the fascists forgot that the Soviet people had only to move a finger, and not a trace of them would be left.

History of the Communist Party of the Soviet Union,
edited by a Commission of the Central Committee
of the Communist Party of the Soviet Union,
Foreign Languages Publishing House Moscow, 1939

Study the last source (D) carefully and then look at the way in which the checklist below has been used to test it for bias and prejudice.

1   *Which words, phrases, and sentences seem to you to be opinions rather than facts (see pages 17–21)?*

'these villains'; 'monstrous moral and political depravity'; 'despicable villainy and treachery'; 'hypocritical professions of loyalty to the Party'; 'gang of assassins and spies'; 'Judas Trotsky'; 'Trotsky-Bukharin fiends'; Whiteguard pigmies, whose strength was no more than that of a gnat'; 'Whiteguard insects'; 'contemptible lackeys of the fascists'.

2   *Are these opinions based on all the facts or only on certain facts which support the opinion in question?*

They appear to be based only on facts extorted by the Secret Police using torture (see Source B).

3   *Does anything in the extract contradict facts which you already know to be true?*

We cannot be absolutely certain that Khruschev (Source B) was telling the whole truth, since he may have been involved in the purges himself. But if his statement is substantially true, then Source D is worthless as a source of accurate information. (It is useful, however, as evidence of the hysterical attitude taken by Soviet Communists during the purges – no doubt anxious to avoid the same fate themselves.)

4 *Does the writer appear to take sides by presenting only one side of an argument or by showing one side only in a favourable or unfavourable light?*

The writer takes one side only – heaping abuse on the so-called enemies of the Soviet people.

5 *Is any part of the extract an obvious lie or exaggeration?*

Almost all of it apart from the dates and names quoted in the extract.

6 *Has the writer used colourful words or phrases to try to influence the way you feel about the facts?*

Yes, throughout – such as 'despicable villainy and treachery'; 'gang of assassins and spies'; 'Judas Trotsky'; 'fiends'; 'Whiteguard pigmies'; 'Whiteguard insects'; and 'contemptible lackeys of the fascists'.

7 *Are any of the statements controversial?*

All of them – according to Khruschev.

EXERCISES AND ACTIVITIES

1 *Examine Sources A, B, C, and D carefully with the aid of the checklist on historical evidence on page 8. Which are primary and which are secondary sources?*

2 *Go through the checklists on pages 18 and 29 with Source A. How does the author differ from the author of Source B in his account of the purges?*

3 *Which parts of Sources A, B, and D do you think are probably accurate and can be accepted as facts?*

4 *Which do you think is the worst example of bias in these extracts?*

5 *Is it possible to think of any Soviet or non-Soviet writer or historian who could give, or have given, an unbiased account of events during the purges? If not, why not?*

6 *Have you enough information to decide for yourself what really happened during the purges? What other sources might you wish to consult to confirm your opinion or to help you make a judgement?*

GAPS AND CONTRADICTIONS

As you have seen, historical sources, both primary and secondary, often contradict each other. Differences of opinion are bound to occur but sources also often disagree about the significance of important facts and events. They are sometimes inconsistent, even contradicting statements made earlier in the same document.

As you have also seen, a source will sometimes leave out inconvenient facts which do not support the opinions or claims of the writer. There may be large gaps in the records. But note that gaps in a source, such as missing days in a diary, can also occur for very simple reasons, such as absence or ill health.

Checklist — Gaps and Contradictions

Here are some of the pointers you can look out for.

1 *Does anything in the extract contradict facts which you know about from other sources? Be careful to distinguish between facts and opinions (see pages 17–21). The contradictions between sources may merely reflect different ways of looking at the same evidence.*

2 *Are there any gaps in the evidence – such as missing dates, facts, or personalities – which support a different version of the events recorded by the writer? If so, is there a good reason for this, such as illness or because these other facts were known only at a later date?*

3 *Is anything in the extract confusing? Does it contradict another part of the same document, for instance by mixing up dates, or people, or the sequence of events?*

4 *Does the writer seek to take credit for successes which other people claim for themselves? Equally, does the writer put the blame for failures on to other people?*

Going through the Checklist

Study Sources A to C which are all about the London Blitz in 1940 and the corresponding British air raids on Berlin at that time. Then go through the checklist with Source C (page 35).

SOURCE A

Saturday, September 7th

Mark this day in your memory. For it has seen the opening of the first serious air attack on London . . .

There stood St Paul's with a semicircular background of red. The flames looked perilously near the dome: while to the left the pall of smoke was black – a dark pillar which drifted uneasily upward.

Anthony Weymouth, *Journal of the War Years,*
Littlebury, 1948

St Paul's Cathedral during the Blitz

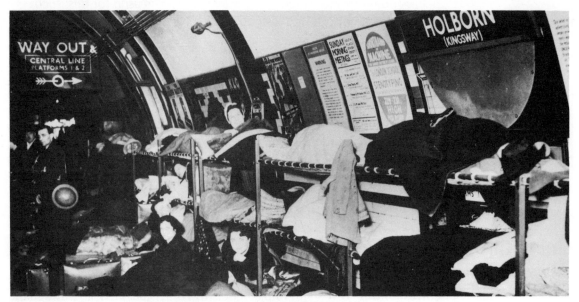

Londoners using the London Underground as an air-raid shelter

SOURCE B

Towards the end of August, the Germans began to supplement their day-time efforts with fairly heavy night attacks and on 24th August a few stray bombs fell on central London. This prompted Churchill to order a retaliation on Berlin on the following night . . .

Apart from its accidental night bombing on 24th August, London was still immune from attack until the afternoon of Saturday, 7th September. I was in my office when the sirens sounded and soon both bombs and machine guns were audible. Since they did not seem to be very near I joined Winterbotham and others on the roof. Against the clear blue sky we could see, away to the east, bombs bursting and smoke billowing from fires in the London docks.

R.V. Jones, *Most Secret War,* Hamish Hamilton, 1978

SOURCE C

BERLIN

September 7

. . . the High Command said in its communiqué today: 'The enemy again attacked the German capital last night, causing some damage to persons and property as a result of his indiscriminate throwing of bombs on non-military targets in the middle of the city. The German air force, as reprisal, has therefore begun to attack London with strong forces.'

Not a hint here – and the German people do not know it – that the Germans have been dropping bombs in the very centre of London for the last two weeks.

September 11

To-day the BBC claims that the Potsdamer station was hit, but this is untrue and at least three Germans to-day who heard the BBC told me they felt a little disillusioned at the BBC radio's lack of veracity [accuracy or honesty]. The point is that it is bad propaganda for the British to broadcast in German to the people here that a main station has been set on fire when it hasn't been touched . . .

William L. Shirer, *Berlin Diary,* Hamish Hamilton 1941
(Shirer was an American journalist
in Berlin between 1934 and 1940.)

1 *Does anything in the extract contradict facts which you know about from the other sources?*

Yes. On 7 September the author says that the Germans have not admitted that they 'have been dropping bombs in the very centre of London for the last two weeks'. This is contradicted by Source A. Anthony Weymouth said that 7 September marked the 'opening of the first serious air attack on London'. Source B confirms this, 'Apart from its accidental night bombing on 24th August, London was still immune from attack until the afternoon of Saturday 7th September.' The reason for the discrepancy, of course, was that Shirer was in Berlin, not London.

2　*Are there any gaps in the evidence – such as missing dates, facts, or personalities – which support a different version of the events recorded by the writer?*

Not so far as we can tell but in wartime all contestants censor information and spread lies about their opponents. Gaps and contradictions are only to be expected.

3　*Is anything in the extract confusing? Does it contradict another part of the same document, for instance by mixing up dates, or people, or the sequence of events?*

No – apart from the question of the raids on London.

4　*Does the writer seek to take credit for successes which other people claim for themselves? Equally, does the writer put the blame for failures on to other people?*

This checkpoint is usually only of relevance in cases where the writer is a participant (like Churchill) rather than an observer (like Shirer).

EXERCISES AND ACTIVITIES

1　*Go through the checklist on page 33 with the other sources (D to K) below. Compare them with Sources A to C. What inconsistencies are there between these different sources?*

2　*What important gap was there in H.C. Knickerbocker's account of the London Blitz which he was going to write for American readers (Source E)? Why was there such a gap? When was this news released to people in Britain?*

3　*What examples of propaganda or misleading information are illustrated in Sources A to K?*

SOURCE D

Weekend: 7–8 September
A special News came over the radio at 10.15 this morning [Sunday], regarding the casualties and damage of the raids. 400 people, at least, were killed in these few hours of air-attacks. It is estimated 1,300–1,400 are seriously injured ... London's Dockland is on fire. Houses galore in the East End are no more.

16 September
We shot down 189 'planes yesterday. We only lost 25 fighters. Magnificent.

Colin Perry, *Boy in the Blitz*, Leo Cooper, 1972

SOURCE E

12th September, 1940
Knickerbocker [an American journalist] dashes up to me aflame with rage. He says he has the best story in the world and the censors are holding it up. It is the story about the time-bomb outside St Paul's Cathedral which may go off at any moment and destroy the great work of Sir Christopher Wren. 'Cannot the American people be brought in to share my anxiety?' Also why is he not allowed to mention the destruction of Bond Street and the Burlington Arcade, so dear to many Americans?

Harold Nicolson, *Diaries and Letters 1939–1945,*
Collins, 1967

SOURCE F

8.0 p.m., Sunday 15 September
John Martin, my Principal Private Secretary, came in with the evening budget of news from all over the world. It was repellent. 'However,' said Martin, as he finished this account, 'all is redeemed by the air. We have shot down one hundred and eighty-three for a loss of under forty.' Although post-war information has shown that the enemy's losses on this day were only fifty-six, September 15 was the crux of the Battle of Britain.

Sir Winston Churchill, *The Second World War:*
Volume 2: Their Finest Hour, Cassell, 1949

SOURCE G

Sunday, September 15th
... we brought down 186 German planes today, for the loss of thirteen pilots, and it looks as if Hitler cannot keep up this pressure for long.

John Colville

London bomb damage

SOURCE H

16 September
Yesterday's battle was immense, with 187 brought down for a loss of no more than 25 British planes and about 12 pilots.

General Raymond E. Lee (US military attaché in London)

SOURCE I

Monday, 16 September
Cabinet in War Room at 12. Not quite so gloomy. Wonderful day in the air yesterday – 185 to 25 (11 pilots safe). Also damage reports not so alarming.

Sir Alexander Cadogan

SOURCE J

GREATEST DAY FOR RAF

Half Raiders Brought Down

350 CAME, ONLY 175 RETURNED

HITLER'S air force returned to mass daylight raids yesterday and the R.A.F. gave them the most shattering defeat they have ever known.

The Air Ministry state that between 350 and 400 enemy aircraft were launched in two waves against London and south-east England.

Of these no fewer than 175 were shot down, four of them by A.A. fire. This is a proportion of nearly one in two destroyed. All these are "certainties," for the total does not include "probables."

The R.A.F. lost 30 'planes, and ten of the pilots are safe.

Most of the raiders that were not destroyed were harassed all the way back to France.

A considerable section of Hitler's invasion fleet in the Channel ports have now been destroyed by the R.A.F.

On Saturday night our bombers gave the invasion ports their most severe battering to date.—See Back Page.

Another Hospital Bombed

PATIENTS SAFE

By Daily Mail Raid Reporter

GERMAN bombers, bound on their nightly terror raiding, arrived at 8.10 last evening.

London's terrific barrage of A.A. guns, stronger than ever at times, forced them to adopt new tactics.

26 FT. DOWN

THIS Daily Mail picture-diagram shows the task that faced the St. Paul's bomb squad. You can see the direction in which the bomb was slipping, 30ft. down, threatening the Cathedral more and more each moment.

They Battled with Ton Time-bomb

ST. PAUL'S IS SAVED BY SIX HEROES

By Daily Mail Reporter

A LITTLE party of experts—an officer, Lieut. R. Davies and five men—have saved St. Paul's Cathedral from almost certain destruction by a gigantic German time-bomb which fell from a 'plane on Thursday and buried itself 26ft. deep in a crater near the walls.

Yesterday at noon, after three days' continuous work, the bomb, 8ft. long, fitted with fuses which made it perilous to handle, was secured by steel tackle and hauled to the surface with a pulley and cable attached to two lorries.

It was one of the biggest that had fallen in London and weighed a ton.

A City fireman who had been on duty continuously in the area told me:

"There were five of them, all young fellows, officered by a French-Canadian. One was an Irishman and a couple came from Yorkshire. Another, I believe, came from Lancashire.

"On the first day they couldn't start work because a six-inch gas-main, broken by the bomb, was blazing. But they've been here from early morning till dusk ever since."

Westminster Abbey Hit

The west window of W............ Abbey was slightly damaged during a recent air-raid.

"The damage was very slight, and only a few small squares were broken," said an official.

Headlines in the Daily Mail, *Monday, 16 September 1940*

SOURCE K

It was hours before Fighter Command knew the extent of their losses – twenty-six planes, thirteen pilots – though the legend of their counter-claim was to persist for many years: a total bag of 183 German planes. Within days, Air Ministry crash investigators had arrived at the truth: the German losses totalled no more than fifty-six, of which thirty-four were bombers.

Richard Collier, *1940 The World In Flames*,
Hamish Hamilton, 1979

EYEWITNESSES AND HEARSAY EVIDENCE

The assassination of President Kennedy at Dallas, Texas, on 22 November 1963. The President has slumped down in his seat and leans towards his wife Jacqueline Kennedy. When you look at a photograph like this you become an eyewitness yourself to one of the dark moments of history.

Eyewitness evidence can take many different forms. A newspaper report, a broadcast, a diary, a photograph, a letter, a television news report, a newsreel film, and a drawing are just some of the different ways in which eyewitnesses have recorded the things they have actually seen or heard. In other words they have witnessed an event or happening with their own eyes and ears. Hence 'eyewitness'. Eyewitnesses can be mistaken but their evidence must be taken seriously if they were really in a position to see or hear something significant.

In a court of law, the evidence from an eyewitness is carefully examined by a judge and by lawyers. It is their job to test the reliability of the witness. They try to make sure that the evidence given is truthful, exact, and accurate. They test the witness to make sure that he or she was not mistaken.

In many cases we cannot question the eyewitnesses who tell us what happened in the past. But we can compare their evidence with other eyewitness accounts and with facts we know about from other sources. We can also use common sense. For instance, how likely is it that someone will have been able to remember the exact words of a conversation which took place fifty years earlier? We ask questions to test the reliability of the evidence to see if the eyewitnesses can really be believed. Was the eyewitness in a good position to see what happened?

Sometimes a source may give the impression that the writer was an eyewitness when in fact the evidence is really based on a report of the incident which the writer heard from someone else. This is called *hearsay evidence*. Witnesses are not usually allowed to use hearsay evidence in a court of law, since there may be no way of checking whether it is accurate.

Hearsay evidence is sometimes used by historians, however, with some reservations. This is because it may have been altered or misunderstood by the person who heard it in the first place. Nonetheless, hearsay evidence is often the only way we have of knowing what went on at a private or secret meeting. For example, you might see something like this in the memoirs of Green:

> I had a long conversation with Black on the 10th. She told me that Brown had stormed out of the Cabinet in a temper.

In other words, Black was the eyewitness *not* Green (i.e. assuming that Black was herself at the Cabinet meeting in question). It would be eyewitness evidence only if Green had been at the Cabinet meeting herself. Instead, it is hearsay evidence and accordingly cannot be entirely trusted since Black could have heard the report from White and White could have heard it from Grey! We have no way of knowing for certain unless the report is backed up by evidence from other sources.

A particular problem with eyewitnesses is the question of when they put their recollections down on paper for the first time or in some other permanent form. You can see a discussion of this in the section on page 63 which deals with memoirs and oral history (spoken recollections of the past).

Although eyewitness evidence has many advantages there is a danger in thinking that an eyewitness must know the truth, or that an eyewitness would not tell a lie. In fact, many eyewitnesses see only a small part of what actually happens. Their evidence is just as liable to bias or distortion as that of writers who were not on the scene at the time of the event.

Checklist — **Evidence from Eyewitnesses**

1 *Does the source indicate in any way that the eyewitness actually saw or experienced the events recorded? We can often find this out from the evidence itself. Look out for clues in the writing which suggest that the writer was actually present, such as the use of 'I' and 'me' – as in 'I saw', 'I heard', 'a woman next to me', 'I tripped and fell'. Other statements may strongly suggest that the writer was an eyewitness, although they could have come from other sources, such as 'the crowd gasped', 'the smell was overpowering'.*

2 *Does the source indicate in any way that it is wholly or partly based on hearsay evidence?*

3 *Is there any clue to show that the eyewitness was in a good position to see what happened?*

4 *Does the evidence justify the actions of the eyewitness in any way? This does not mean that the evidence cannot be trusted, but it does show that the eyewitness is not impartial.*

5 *Are there any other reasons why we may need to treat the evidence of the eyewitness with caution?*

6 *Is there any way of confirming any of the facts described by the eyewitness?*

Going through the Checklist

SOURCE A

THE BATTLE OF EL ALAMEIN
23rd October [1942]

The whole area is now thick with vehicles of various units trying to find their designated locations. A cold wind is blowing in from the sea. I feel rather nervous waiting about in the open – our barrage is due at twenty to ten and then the form will be pretty keen ...

Right on time the barrage bursts, the whole line leaps into life. According to griff [information], it's a record effort: 800 guns of all calibres along the whole Front, one gun every dozen yards, each gun with hundreds of shells. It's certainly a rousing display. The guns nearby crash incessantly, one against another, searing the darkness with gashes of flame, and those farther up and down the line rumble wrathfully and convulse the northern and southern horizons with ceaseless flashing and flickering. Groups of Jock infantry, in shorts and shirts and tin-hats, with bayonets fixed, begin filtering forward through the gap. Poor devils – I don't envy them their night's work. ....

[later the same night]
I get down in the trench also for a spot of kip, while the sergeant minds the phone. But it's hard to sleep. The guns are still bashing away, and now the planes are going over, so that the whole sky is resonant with throbbing and droning. I look straight up into the face of the moon, which is waxen and pallid and wears an expression, so it seems to me, of incredulous dismay at the fantastic scene being enacted down here on this patch of earth.

The Battle of El Alamein

24th October
When the sergeant gently wakes me by the shoulder it's first light, eerily quiet ...

The sergeant tells me the latest news. ... The Jocks have apparently gained all their objectives, and so far there's been no sign of any counter-attack.

Feel a bit more cheerful after a brew and cigarette, and when the sun appears ...

I don't like this place. It's more uncomfortably crowded than ever this morning. Behind us the whole visible desert is cluttered with vehicles, with only a few yards between each, and still more batches coming in. We glare ferociously whenever any newcomers threaten to park too near our trench. What a target for enemy guns, or the Luftwaffe!

R.L. Crimp, *The Diary of a Desert Rat,*
edited by Alex Bowlby, Leo Cooper, 1971

1   *Does the source indicate in any way that the eyewitness actually saw or experienced the events recorded?*

Yes – 'I feel rather nervous waiting about in the open...'

2 *Does the source indicate in any way that it is wholly or partly based on hearsay evidence?*

One sentence only is based on hearsay evidence – 'The sergeant tells me the latest news ... The Jocks have apparently gained all their objectives, and so far there's been no sign of any counter-attack.'

3 *Is there any clue to show that the eyewitness was in a good position to see what happened?*

Yes – 'Behind us the whole visible desert is cluttered with vehicles ...'

4 *Does the evidence justify the actions of the eyewitness in any way?*

No. There are no heroics. For instance, the author is not afraid to say he is 'nervous waiting about in the open'.

5 *Are there any reasons why we may need to treat the evidence of the eyewitness with caution.*

No.

6 *Is there any way of confirming any of the facts described by the eyewitness?*

Only in general – by comparing this account with other descriptions of the start of the battle of El Alamein.

SOURCE B

HAMBURG, 25 July 1943

Back in our flat we stand on the balcony and see nothing but a circle of flames around the Alster, fire everywhere in our neighbourhood. Thick clouds of smoke are hanging over the city, and smoke comes in through all the windows carrying large flakes of fluttering ash ...

There is no proper daylight the following morning, the town is so shrouded in smoke. The sun cannot fight its way through, but looks like a bloodshot eye on to the devastation. It remains like that all through the day; the smell of burning is all-pervading, so are the dust and the ash. And the siren never stops. Maria is in such a state that every time it sounds she makes a dash for the cellar with flying hair and apron strings, and we do not get anything to eat until 5 o'clock after another very heavy day raid, which was worse for the Hahns than for us. Jacoba told us about it afterwards. They cowered in the cellar, Fritz between them, holding a big cushion over his little blond head. The noise was so colossal, and everything shook and trembled so, that they made up their minds there and then: we must get away at once! She telephoned in the evening and told me of their decision; I still thought they were exaggerating and tried to calm her.

Mathilde Wolff-Monckeberg, *On the Other Side*, translated and edited by Ruth Evans, Peter Owen, 1979

Bomb damage in Hamburg

1   *Does the source indicate in any way that the eyewitness actually saw or experienced the events recorded?*

Yes – 'Back in our flat we stand on the balcony and see nothing but a circle of flames around the Alster . . .'

2   *Does the source indicate in any way that it is wholly or partly based on hearsay evidence?*

Partly – the section which begins 'Jacoba told us about it afterwards. They cowered in the cellar, Fritz between them . . .' is hearsay evidence – since the writer heard about it from Jacoba. She did not witness it directly herself.

3   *Is there any clue to show that the eyewitness was in a good position to see what happened?*

Yes – 'we stand on the balcony and see nothing but a circle of flames . . .'

4   *Does the evidence justify the actions of the eyewitness in any way?*

No.

5   *Are there any reasons why we may need to treat the evidence of the eyewitness with caution?*

No.

6   *Is there any way of confirming any of the facts described by the eyewitness?*

Only by comparing this account with similar descriptions of the same air raid from similar sources.

EXERCISES AND ACTIVITIES

1   *Use the checklist on pages 40–1 to go through the following extract. In it a Chinese official tells an American journalist about his experiences during Mao Zedong's Cultural Revolution (1965–8).*

'First of all,' he said, 'you can't imagine how exciting it all was. Every morning, you came to your office. You could hardly wait to get there to see what was new, to see what the new posters said....

You never knew when you yourself might be attacked. Often you and your comrades would make up a Big Character poster attacking someone in the morning, and in the afternoon another poster would denounce that of the morning. It was a continuous fever. Everyone was swept up in it. There were meetings in the Tien-an Men. Something was happening all the time.'...

Officials, party members, bureaucrats, members of the party apparatus were sent to live in the country to work with their hands, to 'cleanse their thought', to get back to Marxist and Maoist fundamentals. Everyone went...

They built their own huts with crude brick or baked mud walls. They broke ground, planted crops, irrigated the land. They worked to exhaustion and suffered freezing cold in winter and the blazing-oven heat of China's summer. 'It was a wonderful experience,' the official said. 'It was the great experience of my life ... Now I know what life in China means.'

Harrison E. Salisbury, *To Peking – And Beyond*,
Arrow Books, 1973

2   *Would you have enjoyed taking part in Mao Zedong's Cultural Revolution? If not, why not? Why do you think it is important to know something about the eyewitness when you read an eyewitness account?*

3   *What was the Chinese official getting at when he said 'Now I know what life in China means'?*

Different Types of Historical Evidence

RELICS FROM THE PAST

Some of the relics from the past which we can see and touch are called *archaeological remains*. Archaeology is the science which studies the past through the materials left behind by people in the past. Much of what we know from archaeology has been discovered by unearthing pottery, tools, bones, and the remains of buildings buried in the ground. Thirty years ago people thought of archaeology as being concerned only with prehistory – the period before there were written documents to tell us about past events and past peoples. This has changed. Nowadays archaeologists study the recent past as well as the distant past. Industrial archaeology in particular, is concerned with the tools, machines, engines, mills, and early factories which marked the beginnings of the Industrial and Agricultural Revolutions.

Checklist — **Relics from the Past**

Studying the past at a site such as a battlefield, or in a museum, or from photographs can be a very useful way of backing up what you know about modern world history from other historical sources, like documents. If you do make such a study, this checklist may be useful in helping you to find out more about the subject.

1 *What was the purpose of the object or building you are studying? What was it used for? Why was it built or made?*

2 *Can you date the object or building either exactly or approximately?*

3 *Where is it situated now or where was it found? Where did it come from originally?*

4 *What does it tell us about people in the past?*

Going through the Checklist

Look at these photographs and then work through the checklist.

Fragment from a German Zeppelin located in the porch of Theberton Church in Suffolk

Memorial plaque in the churchyard at Theberton in Suffolk

> **HERE WERE BURIED 16 GERMAN AIRMEN CREW OF ZEPPELIN L 48 17ᵀᴴ JUNE 1917 "WHO ART THOU THAT JUDGEST ANOTHER MANS SERVANT." ROM. XIV-IV.**

1 *What was the purpose of the object or building you are studying? What was it used for? Why was it built or made?*

German airships, or Zeppelins, were used as bombers during the First World War.

2 *Can you date the object or building either exactly or approximately?*

Yes, approximately. It was built before June 1917 – probably in the period 1914–17.

3 *Where is it situated now or where was it found? Where did it come from originally?*

The fragment of the Zeppelin is situated now at Theberton Church in Suffolk close to the place where the Zeppelin crashed in June 1917. It came originally from an airfield in Germany.

4 *What does it tell us about people in the past?*

It tells us that the crew of a Zeppelin consisted of at least 16 airmen. It also shows that people in Britain could still treat their enemies with respect in June 1917 at a time when most families had already lost brothers, fathers, or uncles in the fighting.

EXERCISES AND ACTIVITIES

Look at these photographs of war memorials to British servicemen, built at the end of the First World War. What do these memorials tell you about the First World War? Are there any memorials like these in your town?

Simple wooden crosses from Flanders on a wall in Salisbury Cathedral

War memorial in the centre of Newcastle upon Tyne

Royal Artillery war memorial, Hyde Park Corner, London

DOCUMENTARY EVIDENCE

Anything that is written down (such as a letter), or printed (such as a newspaper) is called *documentary evidence*. It includes wills, Acts of Parliament, advertisements, posters, timetables, receipts, letters, journals, diaries, and anything else in written or printed form.

```
                                    Sunday,
                                    7th December, 1941.
                                    Midnight.

        Here is the News, and this is Alvar Lidell reading it.

        Japan's long-threatened aggression in the Far East began

   tonight with air attacks on United States naval bases in the

   Pacific.   Fresh reports are coming in every minute; the latest

   facts the situation are these:-

             The Japanese air raids were made on the Hawaiian islands

   and the Philippines;  observers' reports say that an American

   battleship has been hit, and that a number of the Japanese bombers

   have been shot down.   A naval action is in progress off Honolulu;

   an American transport with timber on board has been torpedoed in

   the Pacific, and another cargo ship is reported in distress.

   President Roosevelt has told the Army and Navy to act on their

   secret orders, has called a meeting of Ministers, and is preparing

   a report for Congress.   In London, Mr. Winant has seen Mr.Churchill,

   and both Houses of Parliament have been summoned for tomorrow

   afternoon to hear a statement on the situation.   Messages

   from Tokio say that Japan has announced a formal declaration of war

   against both the United States and Britain.
```

The script of the BBC news bulletin announcing the Japanese attack on Pearl Harbor in 1941

The first thing you should do when you see documentary evidence like this is to read it through carefully to make sure you understand what it means. Then examine it closely to see how far you can trust it as a reliable piece of historical evidence. You can do this with the aid of the master checklist which follows. As you can see, it combines the earlier checklists printed on pages 8 (historical evidence), 18 (facts and opinions), 22 (accuracy and reliability), and 29 (bias and prejudice), 33 (gaps and contradictions), 40–1 (eyewitnesses). It is also printed at the back of the book on page 131 as a convenient source of reference. When you use this master checklist, ignore checkpoints which are irrelevant to the extract you are studying or for which you have insufficient information to make a sensible response.

Master Checklist — **Documentary Evidence**

1 *What does the source tell you about the past?*

2 *What is the origin of the source? What type of evidence is it (e.g. diary, letter, newspaper report)? Is it likely to be reliable?*

3 *Why was the source written? Was it written to justify the writer's actions? Does the writer try to take credit for successes which other people claim for themselves? Does the writer put the blame for failures on to other people?*

4 *When was the source written? Is it a primary source dating from the time of the event which it describes? Or is it a secondary source?*

5 *Is there any clue or statement to show that it is an actual eyewitness account? Was the writer in a good position to say what happened? Does the source agree with other eyewitness accounts of the same event? Are there any reasons for thinking the eyewitness cannot be trusted entirely?*

6 *If the source was written years after the event, is there any reason to doubt the accuracy of the writer's memory?*

7 *Which parts of the extract seem to you to be opinions and not facts which can be proved right or wrong? Are the opinions based on facts or on prejudice? Has the writer used words of approval or disapproval, or colourful or exaggerated phrases, to try to influence the reader?*

8 *Does the author show any other signs of bias or prejudice? Does the writer appear to take sides in an argument?*

9 *Are there any obvious mistakes or errors of fact in the extract? Which statements are supported by facts you know about from other sources? Does anything in the extract contradict other sources, or facts which you already know to be true?*

10 *Does the account give a distorted view of events which actually occurred? Has the author left out facts which tell a different story? Is any part of the extract an obvious lie or exaggeration? Are there any obvious gaps in the evidence, such as missing dates, facts, or personalities?*

Going through the Checklist

Here is an example of the way in which the master checklist can be used to evaluate a historical source. It describes a private meeting in Munich between the British prime minister, Neville Chamberlain, and the German dictator, Adolf Hitler, at the time of the signing of the Munich Agreement in 1938.

SOURCE A

Letter from Neville Chamberlain (British prime minister)
to his two sisters: 2 October 1938

I asked Hitler about 1 in the morning [on 30 September], while we were waiting for the draftsmen, whether he would care to see me for another talk. He jumped at the idea, and asked me to come to his private flat, in a tenement house where the other floors are occupied by ordinary citizens. I had a very friendly and pleasant talk: on Spain (where he too said he had never had any territorial ambitions), economic relations with SE Europe, and disarmament. I did not mention colonies, nor did he. At the end I pulled out the declaration, which I had prepared beforehand, and asked if he would sign it. As the interpreter translated the words into German, Hitler frequently ejaculated *'Ja, Ja,'* and at the end he said 'Yes, I will certainly sign it; when shall we do it?' I said 'Now', and we went at once to the writing-table, and put our signatures to the two copies which I had brought with me.

K. Feiling, *The Life of Neville Chamberlain*,
Macmillan, 1946

1 *What does the source tell you about the past?*

It explains the circumstances which enabled Neville Chamberlain to get Hitler to sign the notorious document (Source B) which asserted 'the desire of our two peoples never to go to war with one another again'. On 1 October 1938, Chamberlain said of this document, 'I believe it is peace for our time'. Eleven months later he declared war on Germany.

2 *What is the origin of the source? What type of evidence is it (e.g. diary, letter, newspaper report)? Is it likely to be reliable?*

It is a private letter, from the British prime minister to his two sisters, giving a personal account of his private meeting with Hitler. At first sight it looks as if it must be the only authoritative source of information in English of what actually happened, since Hitler left no documents to confirm or deny Chamberlain's account of the meeting. However, there was someone else present at that meeting – 'the interpreter' who 'translated the words into German'. Hitler's interpreter was Dr Paul Schmidt and he later wrote his own account of this meeting (Source C below). As you will see it does not confirm Chamberlain's impression of 'a very friendly and pleasant talk'.

3 *Why was the source written? Was it written to justify the writer's actions? Does the writer try to take credit for successes which other people claim for themselves? Does the writer put the blame for failures on to other people?*

It justifies – or, at least, explains – the actions of the British prime minister, since they were, and still are, a matter of great controversy.

4 *When was the source written? Is it a primary source dating from the time of the event which it describes? Or is it a secondary source?*

It was written only two days after the event, so it is a primary source.

5 *Is there any clue or statement to show that it is an actual eyewitness account? Was the writer in a good position to say what happened?*

It is obviously an actual eyewitness account. The writer was in a good position to say what happened at the meeting. But he did not speak German fluently enough to speak directly to Hitler. Consequently the interpreter, who spoke both English and German, was in an even better position to say what happened (Source C).

6 *If the source was written years after the event is there any reason to doubt the accuracy of the writer's memory?*

This checkpoint does not apply since it was written only two days after the meeting.

7 *Which parts of the extract seem to you to be opinions and not facts which can be proved right or wrong?*

(a) That Hitler 'jumped at the idea' of signing the celebrated peace declaration.
(b) That Chamberlain and Hitler 'had a very friendly and pleasant talk'.

8 *Does the author show any other signs of bias or prejudice? Does the writer appear to take sides in an argument?*

No.

9 *Are there any obvious mistakes or errors of fact in the extract? Which statements are supported by facts you know about from other sources? Does anything in the extract contradict other sources, or facts which you already know to be true?*

No. The fact that the meeting took place in Hitler's house, the general topics of conversation, and the circumstances surrounding the signing of the 'piece of paper' are confirmed by Dr Paul Schmidt (Hitler's interpreter) in Source C (below).

10 *Does the account give a distorted view of events which actually occurred?*

Not as far as we can tell from the extract on its own. But Chamberlain took a much more optimistic view of Hitler's attitude than Hitler's own interpreter did (see Source C below). Dr Paul Schmidt thought that Hitler looked 'pale and moody' and that he only 'listened absent-mindedly' to Chamberlain and contributed 'little to the conversation'. The interpreter did not agree that Hitler was keen to sign the declaration. 'My own feeling was that he agreed to the wording with a certain reluctance and I believe he appended his signature only to please Chamberlain.' Bear in mind, of course, that these are differences of opinion, and not differences of fact.

SOURCE B

> We, the German Führer and Chancellor and the British Prime Minister, have had a further meeting today and are agreed in recognising that the question of Anglo-German relations is of the first importance for the two countries and for Europe.
>
> We regard the agreement signed last night and the Anglo-German Naval Agreement as symbolic of the desire of our two peoples never to go to war with one another again.
>
> We are resolved that the method of consultation shall be the method adopted to deal with any other questions that may concern our two countries, and we are determined to continue our efforts to remove possible sources of difference and thus to contribute to assure the peace of Europe.

September 30. 1938 -

The 'piece of paper' which Neville Chamberlain proudly displayed on his return to Britain after his meeting with Hitler

Neville Chamberlain at Heston Airport waving the 'piece of paper'

EXERCISES AND ACTIVITIES

SOURCE C

There was only a brief rest after the signing of the Agreement, for the next morning I was at Hitler's house to interpret the conversation with Chamberlain. Hitler looked quite different as he sat beside me, pale and moody. He listened absent-mindedly to Chamberlain's remarks about Anglo–German relations, disarmament and economic questions, contributing comparatively little to the conversation. Towards the end of the conversation Chamberlain drew the famous Anglo–German Declaration from his pocket ... Slowly, emphasising each word, I translated this statement to Hitler.

I did not share Chamberlain's impression, expressed in a private letter of his now published, that Hitler eagerly assented to this declaration. My own feeling was that he agreed to the wording with a certain reluctance, and I believe he appended his signature only to please Chamberlain, without promising himself any too much from the effects of the declaration.

Dr Paul Schmidt, *Hitler's Interpreter*,
edited by R. H. C. Steed, Heinemann, 1951

1   *Use the checklist on page 51 to test this document. In particular take careful note of the balance between facts and opinions in this account of a very important meeting.*

2   *You probably have as much evidence as any historian can have of what happened at this private meeting between Hitler and Chamberlain. Write an account of this meeting using the facts which are common to both sources and explain the different ways in which the two participants (Chamberlain and Schmidt) describe Hitler's attitude to the meeting.*

NEWSPAPERS AND MAGAZINES

NIXON RESIGNS

HE URGES A TIME OF 'HEALING'; FORD WILL TAKE OFFICE TODAY

'Sacrifice' Is Praised; Kissinger to Remain

By ANTHONY RIPLEY
Special to The New York Times

WASHINGTON, Aug. 8—Vice President Ford praised President Nixon - tonight for "one of the greatest personal sacrifices for the country and one of the finest personal decisions on behalf of all of us as Americans."

Mr. Ford, who will take office as the 38th President at noon tomorrow, vowed to continue Mr. Nixon's foreign policy and announced that Secretary of State Kissinger had agreed to stay on in the new Administration.

"I pledge to you tonight, as

SPECULATION RIFE ON VICE PRESIDENT

Some Ford Associates Say Selecting a Successor Could Take Weeks

I will pledge to you tomorrow and in the future, my best efforts for cooperation, leadership and dedication to what's good for America and good for the world," he said.

The Vice President, who never sought the nation's highest office and disclaimed any intention of seeking it after Mr. Nixon's term, will take the oath of office in a private ceremony at the White House.

Thus will he become the first man to serve as President without being chosen by the American people in an election. Tomorrow night he will address the nation on radio and television. It is expected that he will speak at 6 P.M.

All day today the signs of the historic change were in the air, sensed by the crowds that gathered along Pennsylvania

Text of Mr. Ford's remarks appears on Page 7.

Avenue near the White House.

The New York Times/William E. Sauro
Vice President Ford meeting with newsmen last night

United Press International
President Nixon on TV as he announced his resignation

The 37th President Is First to Quit Post

By JOHN HERBERS
Special to The New York Times

WASHINGTON, Aug. 8—Richard Milhous Nixon, the 37th President of the United States, announced tonight that he had given up his long and arduous fight to remain in office and would resign, effective at noon tomorrow.

At that hour, Gerald Rudolph Ford, whom Mr. Nixon nominated for Vice President last Oct. 12, will be sworn in as the 38th President, to serve out the 895 days remaining in Mr. Nixon's second term.

Less that two years after his landslide re-election victory, Mr. Nixon, in a conciliatory address on national

Text of the address will be found on Page 2.

television, said that he was leaving not with a sense of bitterness but with a hope that his departure would start a "process of healing that is so desperately needed in America."

He spoke of regret for any "injuries" done "in the course of the events that led to this decision." He acknowledged that some of his judgments had been wrong.

The 61-year-old Mr. Nixon, appearing calm and resigned to his fate as a victim of the Watergate scandal, became the first President in the history of the Republic to resign from office. Only 10 months earlier Spiro Agnew resigned the Vice-Presidency.

Speaks of Pain at Yielding Post

| POLITICAL SCENE SHARPLY ALTERED | *Rise and Fall* Appraisal of Nixon Career | JAWORSKI ASSERTS NO DEAL WAS MADE |

Front page of The New York Times, 9 August 1974. Who was Nixon and why did he resign?

The first popular British newspaper, the *Daily Mail*, cost a halfpenny (about 0.2p) when it was first published in 1896. Since then many other popular cheap newspapers have been published as well, including the *Daily Express* (1900), *Daily Mirror* (1904), and the *Sun* (1969). The first illustrated weekly magazines were begun in the middle of the nineteenth century with the founding of *The Illustrated London News* and the humorous weekly *Punch*. Many of these magazines and newspapers relied on advertisements so that they could be sold cheaply. Old newspapers and magazines are an invaluable source of historical evidence. Some, such as *The Times* have been copied on to microfilm.

The great advantage of newspapers and magazines as historical sources is that they were written at the time as contemporary news reports. So they are primary historical sources. They were also written for ordinary people to read, so they are often more interesting and easier to read than official documents. This is not to say that they are always to be trusted. Far from it. Many news reports were based on hearsay evidence, on biased reports from prejudiced journalists, or even taken straight from the columns of other newspapers. There is often no way of knowing what has been left out of a report or how reliable the anonymous writer was. Opinions are sometimes quoted as if they were facts. Many newspapers were (and still are) biased in favour of a particular political party. Popular newspapers often distort or colour the facts in order to make a news story more interesting to their readers.

AEROPLANE DROPS A
BOMB ON DOVER.

EXPLOSION IN GARDEN.

NO DAMAGE DONE.

PURSUIT IN FOG BY BRITISH
AIRCRAFT.

THE WAR OFFICE ANNOUNCES:

An enemy aeroplane was seen over Dover this morning about 10.55. It dropped a bomb, which fell in a garden and exploded, but did no damage.

The aeroplane was only seen for a few seconds, and lost again over sea.

British aircraft went up at once, but did not see the enemy again. The weather was foggy and cloudy.

This first authenticated instance of an air raid on these shores —there have been rumours in plenty—comes just five and a half years after the great day (July, 1909) when a Frenchman first accomplished the feat of flying across the Channel.

Assuming that a German aeroplane would start from Ostend, the distance from that point to Dover as the crow flies would be about seventy miles.

Probable Route.

News item from The Star *for 24 December 1914. What was the particular significance of this air raid?*

EXERCISES AND ACTIVITIES

GREAT ARMADA ATTACKS

4,000   Ships,   With   Several   Thousand   Smaller   Craft,   Cross   The   Channel

CHURCHILL TELLS THE HOUSE

Hopes Of Tactical Surprise

WHAT THE PREMIER SAID

Announcing the landings on the European Continent to an excited House to-day, Mr. Churchill said: "An immense armada of upwards of 4,000 ships with several thousand smaller craft have crossed the Channel."

Massed airborne landings had been successfully effected behind the enemy's lines, the Premier added.

The landings on the beaches were proceeding at various points at the present time. The fire of the shore batteries had been largely quelled.

The obstacles which were constructed in the sea had not proved to be as difficult as was apprehended.

The Anglo-American Allies were sustained by about 11,000 first-line aircraft, which could be drawn upon as might be needed for the purposes of the battle.

TACTICAL SURPRISE?

"There are already hopes that actual tactical surprise has been attained, and we hope to furnish the enemy with a succession of surprises during the course of the fighting."

NEW LANDINGS IN CHANNEL ISLES, SAYS BERLIN

SIGNIFICANT FACTS RELATING TO THE GREAT ALLIED OPERATIONS FOR THE LIBERATION OF EUROPE WERE GIVEN BY MR. CHURCHILL IN THE COMMONS TO-DAY. "THERE ARE ALREADY HOPES THAT ACTUAL TACTICAL SURPRISE HAS BEEN ATTAINED, AND WE HOPE TO FURNISH THE ENEMY WITH A SUCCESSION OF SURPRISES DURING THE COURSE OF THE FIGHTING," HE SAID.

Among the facts which Mr. Churhill gave the House were: An immense armada of upwards of 4,000 ships, with several thousand smaller craft have crossed the Channel. Massed airborne landings have been successfully effected behind the enemy lines. Landings on beaches are proceeding at various points. The fire of shore batteries has been "largely quelled." The Allies are sustained by about 11,000 first-line aircraft.

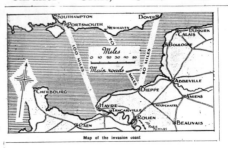

Map of the invasion coast

Headlines in the Nottingham Evening Post *for 6 June 1944*

1   *What was the 'Great Armada' and why and what did it attack? Find out if the map printed in the newspaper was accurate or not.*

2   *Why were the evening papers able to beat the daily papers at being first to print the news of this great event?*

Look at the cuttings opposite from three newspapers printed during the General Strike in May 1926.

3   *Go through each of these sources with the aid of the master checklist on page 51.*

4   *Which of these newspapers show political bias and in which direction? How do they try to convince their readers?*

5   *Compare the different ways in which all three newspapers appear to suggest that they know what the attitude of the general public was to the Strike.*

6   *Which newspaper would you have chosen to read had you wanted an unbiased account of the General Strike?*

A food convoy during the General Strike

SOURCE B

The British Worker,
Monday, 10 May 1926

NATION BEHIND THE T.U.C.

What a London Park Meeting Revealed

£55 COLLECTION

The quiet determination of the men on strike has impressed the outside public. The strikers' confidence and enthusiasm are contagious. They have spread to other sections of the nation.

"They don't look a bit like unemployed," remarked a young woman onlooker, who stood on the step of a West Norwood villa while a procession of transport strikers, be-medalled and in Sunday attire, marched in fours to Brockwell Park.

The immense crowd in the park gave a clear indication of where the sympathies of the British nation lie in this dispute. Many of the crowd were trade unionists, including strikers and their families, but at least a third of them were of the class which the Press loves to call "the general public" — bank and insurance clerks, small shopkeepers, holders of season-tickets, dwellers in suburban villas.

SOURCE A

Daily Mail, Wednesday,
5 May 1926

Yesterday the general strike came into force, showing that there is no extremity of violence from which the persons behind this conspiracy will shrink. Their ostensible leaders, the Parliamentary politicians - whose business it is to act the role of decoy ducks and win the support of the muddle-headed and simple - may deal in sobstuff about the "terrible situation", and their reluctance to go to extremes. But while they talk, their followers act. While the House of Commons is treated to lacrimose speeches, the country is being "held up".

The British nation is eager to support its Government. It is waiting for its Government to act. It is looking to its Government to act. It is capable of any effort and of any sacrifice. But a nation cannot rally unless there is action; it cannot feel enthusiasm for a policy of sitting still. It never admired the policy of Kerensky, whose fault it was to imagine that words were the equivalent of deeds. When a fight is in progress (and the leaders of this strike have not hesitated to use the word "war") the only thing to do is to win it, not to think of what will happen if we do not win it. That is the policy which caused the failure of Jutland.

THE END OF THE GENERAL STRIKE.

QUESTIONS OF PRAISE AND BLAME.

Everybody's first thought to-day must be one of profound satisfaction that the general strike is over. The British people have come with credit out of a severe ordeal. During an unprecedented struggle, extending over nine days, not a cartridge—not even a blank cartridge—has been fired by a soldier, and no single fatal colli sion has occurred between the strikers and the civil power. There has been no food shortage, no panic, and wonderfully little loss of temper on either side. In a fair trial of strength, which we hope may never be repeated, the nation has stood up to the general strike and overcome it.

Trade unionists, we believe, will agree that the calling of the general strike was a serious blunder. It placed their movement in a false position. Mr. Lloyd George, in a message sent out early yesterday before the settlement, stated the matter in two sentences. "If," he said,

"The trade unions inflict a defeat on the Government, it will be an encouragement to the extreme elements in Labour to resort in future to the general strike as a weapon of offence, whenever they find their purpose thwarted by the normal working of democratic institutions. Such a defeat would sooner or later end the experiment of popular government in these islands."

The time will come later to review the situation fully, and to decide the respective responsibilities of the Government and the T.U.C., but some things are clear already. The Government committed a disastrous blunder, when on the night of Sunday, May 2, after its basis for continuing to treat with its miners had been actually accepted by the T.U.C., it abruptly banged the door on negotiations. But for that, it seems certain that a settlement would have been reached without a strike. There was nothing unusual in it being deferred to the final 24 hours; settlements very often are. What was unusual, was that, by the Government's folly, the final 24 hours were suddenly made unavailable for negotiation. Mr. Baldwin has never been a cheap Prime Minister, but this was one of his costliest mistakes.

SOURCE C

The Daily Chronicle,
Thursday, 13 May 1926

JOURNALS, DIARIES AND LETTERS

Travel journals, diaries, and letters are an important source of historical evidence. This is because they are primary sources. The descriptions are usually eyewitness accounts, and the writers often recall conversations which were still fresh in the mind when they wrote them. The more interesting personal diaries and journals have been published, since they are an invaluable source of information for historians. The most famous daily journal is probably the *Diary of Samuel Pepys* which was written in the 1660s. Diaries which have been published recently include those by four Labour party cabinet ministers – Hugh Gaitskell, Richard Crossman, Barbara Castle, and Tony Benn – describing events of the 1950s, 1960s, and 1970s.

The diary entries you will see will probably fall into two main groups. The first group contains the many diaries which have been published primarily because the diarist is or was someone famous (such as Dr Goebbels) or close to someone famous, such as an interpreter, husband or wife, or a private secretary (like Frances Stevenson – see page 15).

The second group contains diaries which have been published because they throw unusual or fascinating light on the past through the eyes of ordinary people with no particular claim to fame. These diaries are almost always interesting and provide a valuable source of information about everyday life in the past. For instance, many diaries have been published which show what ordinary people thought and felt during the Second World War, such as Colin Perry's wartime diary *Boy in the Blitz* describing the German air raids on London in 1940 (see page 36) and the similar diary by Mathilde Wolff-Monckeberg, *On the Other Side*, which describes the Allied air raids on Hamburg (see page 43).

Collections of letters written by famous people, such as the private letters of Neville Chamberlain to his two sisters (see page 52) have also been published. These are particularly useful where the letters are addressed to other important people and their replies have been published as well, such as those between the American President Franklin Roosevelt and other statesmen, such as Winston Churchill. Letters between statesmen and politicians often help historians to discover the reasons why actions were taken in the past. It helps us to understand their motives.

At first glance, journals, diaries, and letters seem to be an ideal historical source. Those by famous people are often especially interesting where they tell us why certain actions were taken, and what the writer thought as well as what he or she did. But there are a number of drawbacks. Famous people know that their letters and diaries will probably be published for everyone to read. This is why they are often written as if the writer is attempting to justify or excuse certain actions. It is difficult to be certain that the writer is being honest. The diaries of ordinary people are often more revealing. Samuel Pepys tells far more in his diary than he told people to their faces. It is also a fact that the participants at a meeting can often come away with very different impressions (as you saw when Chamberlain met Hitler in 1938 – see pages 52–5). The extract which follows is taken from a diary by an American journalist who was in charge of the foreign service of the *The New York Times*. In his job he met most of the world's leading politicians and statesmen of the 1930s, 1940s and 1950s.

> ... in contemplating my own diary, I remember how inaccurate diaries can be. Once I played cards with Eisenhower, Harriman, Gruenther and Dan Kimball, United States Secretary of the Navy, while all discussed the memoirs of James Forrestal, first Secretary of Defence. They had attended a meeting referred to in the book and each agreed that Forrestal's account was wrong. But when I asked what, then, was the true version, all promptly disagreed among themselves.
>
> C. L. Sulzberger, *A Long Row of Candles:*
> *Memoirs and Diaries 1934–1954*, Macdonald, 1969

EXERCISES AND ACTIVITIES

The following letter (or memorandum) was written by President Roosevelt on 1 December 1941 and sent to Cordell Hull, his Secretary of State (the American minister in charge of foreign affairs). It was written just six days before the Japanese attacked Pearl Harbor.

> THE WHITE HOUSE
> DEC. 1, 1941
>
> Memorandum for the Secretary of State
>
> I have received reports during the past days of continuing Japanese troop movements to southern Indo-China [now Vietnam]. These reports indicate a very rapid and material increase in the forces of all kinds stationed by Japan in Indo-China. ...
>
> Please be good enough to request the Japanese Ambassador and Ambassador Kurusu to inquire at once of the Japanese Government what the actual reasons may be for the steps already taken, and what I am to consider is the policy of the Japanese Government as demonstrated by this recent and rapid concentration of troops in Indo-China. ...
>
> F.D.R.

Japanese troops in
South East Asia, 1941

1 What does this letter tell you about America's relations with Japan in the weeks before Pearl Harbor?

2 What is the particular value of this letter when compared with an account of the war against Japan in a history textbook?

3 Use the checklist on page 51 to examine the further extract from C. L. Sulzberger's diary which is printed below. What does it tell you about the postwar history of Japan?

TOKYO
May 17, 1950

I am amazed at the recovery of Tokyo. Today when you drive around you would never know there had been a war – at least in the part I have visited. All the main buildings in the financial centre are untouched and the little shacks which are normal in Japanese cities have been completely reconstructed. Tokyo is a bustling, hardworking city and it is clear that at least on the surface American influence is strong. Most people now wear European clothes and the women wander about on the same free and easy basis as Western women, even though some of them still wear kimonos and wooden shoes.

MEMOIRS AND ORAL HISTORY

Oral history is spoken history. It is recollections about the past which are told to a historian rather than written down as memoirs. Oral history is usually first recorded on cassette, tape, or video but may be written down at a later date. Oral historians record the reminiscences of ordinary people rather than those of the famous, such as a former coal miner talking about the General Strike in 1926 and the suffragette describing life in prison. Everyone has listened to oral history like this, even if it is only a grandparent talking about the 1930s or parents describing their own schooldays.

Nowadays historians recognise that oral history can make a big contribution to our understanding of the past. It is also a method of writing history which is open to anyone who has a cassette recorder.

Memoirs, on the other hand, are usually written by people of importance, such as a former prime minister or an admiral. The main difference compared with oral history is that they are written down instead of being spoken. They are almost always backed up in detail by documentary evidence, such as diaries, letters, and official documents.

Both types of recollection – the spoken history and the written memoir – may be inaccurate and unreliable historical sources. This is because they depend heavily on human memory, which may or may not be faulty. Older people often tend to remember the past as being either much better or much worse than the present. Only rarely do they seem to think of it as being the same! If people were poor, they were much poorer than today. If they were happy, they were much happier than today! Not surprisingly, people recalling past events tend to justify their own actions. Writers of memoirs may skip over their mistakes and omit the less successful, or more shameful periods of their lives. Above all, beware of the razor-sharp recollection of events which happened fifty or sixty years ago. This is not eyewitness evidence you can always trust.

EXERCISES AND ACTIVITIES

Use a cassette recorder to make an oral history which you can use when you study a topic in modern world history, such as the General Strike in 1926, evacuation during the Second World War, the Blitz, the Cuba Crisis of 1962, the referendum on Britain's entry into the European Economic Community in 1975, or the miners' strike of 1984–5. Choose a theme which your older relatives can talk about. When you have made the tape recording use the master checklist on page 51 to test the reliability of your historical sources.

USING PROPAGANDA AND ADVERTS

Propaganda is anything which deliberately sets out to persuade you to accept only one particular viewpoint, attitude, or set of facts, irrespective of the truth. At its worst it is a campaign by ruthless people, such as the Nazis, to distort the truth in order to win backing for a war or a campaign of persecution. At its best, it is an effective advertisement designed to persuade people to give up a habit, such as cigarette smoking, which experts believe could damage their health. Nowadays television is the most powerful medium through which to advertise or disseminate propaganda. The Nazi minister for propaganda, Dr Josef Goebbels, recognised the power of broadcasting in the 1930s, long before it was effectively used in Britain or America.

German poster of the 1930s – 'ONE PEOPLE – ONE COUNTRY – ONE LEADER'

'All Germany hears the Führer with the People's Radio'

Propaganda is a valuable source of historical evidence, since it often tells us a lot about the way in which the great dictators of the twentieth century held on to power and how they managed to get popular support for their policies. Posters, advertisements, broadcasts, films, official publications, and speeches helped to surround the leader – Führer, Duce, or Caudillo – with an almost religious atmosphere of mystery, awe, and power. Mussolini revered the days of the ancient Roman Empire when Italy dominated Europe, North Africa and the Middle East. This is why the Fascists deliberately chose the ancient Roman symbol of authority – the *fasces* (a bundle of rods grouped around an axe) as their symbol of power. Mussolini liked to speak to a crowd standing in front of a classical building or statue. The Fascist salute – the upraised arm – was used by soldiers in Ancient Rome. You can see this theme repeated time and again in Fascist propaganda, such as a poster showing the Italian army marching into Abyssinia with Roman legions supporting them in the background.

What does this photograph tell you about Mussolini and the Italian Fascists?

The Nazis used simple propaganda slogans to portray Hitler as a Messiah who had come to save Germany. In 1937 Dr Ley, a leading Nazi politician, was quoted as telling an audience:

> Everything comes from Adolf Hitler. His faith is our faith, and therefore our daily prayer is: I believe in Adolf Hitler alone!

Rudolf Hess (Hitler's deputy) in his Christmas speech on 24 December 1940 went even further:

> On this Christmas, our prayer is: 'Lord Almighty, Thou hast given us the Führer: Thou hast blessed his struggle by a mighty victory . . .'

EXERCISES AND ACTIVITIES

1 *What was the propaganda message conveyed to the Russian people by this sculpture entitled 'The struggle for peace'? How does it depict Stalin?*

British advertisement in December 1914 aimed at people wealthy enough to employ servants

5 Questions to those who employ male servants

1. HAVE you a Butler, Groom, Chauffeur, Gardener, or Gamekeeper serving you who, at this moment should be serving your King and Country ?

2. Have you a man serving at your table who should be serving a gun ?

3. Have you a man digging your garden who should be digging trenches ?

4. Have you a man driving your car who should be driving a transport wagon ?

5. Have you a man preserving your game who should be helping to preserve your Country ?

A great responsibility rests on you. Will you sacrifice your personal convenience for your Country's need ?

Ask your men to enlist TO-DAY.

The address of the nearest Recruiting Office can be obtained at any Post Office.

God Save the King.

2 *What does this advertisement tell you about Britain in 1914? Who was being asked to make a sacrifice?*

3 *How does this famous 'Wanted' poster make its point? Why do you think it was published? Does it tell us anything about the causes of the Second World War?*

WANTED!

FOR MURDER . . . FOR KIDNAPPING . . . FOR THEFT AND FOR ARSON

Can be recognised full face by habitual scowl. Rarely smiles. Talks rapidly, and when angered screams like a child.

ADOLF HITLER
ALIAS
Adolf Schicklegruber, Adolf Hittler or Hidler

Last heard of in Berlin, September 3, 1939. Aged fifty, height 5ft. 8½in., dark hair, frequently brushes one lock over left forehead. Blue eyes. Sallow complexion, stout build, weighs about 11st. 3lb. Suffering from acute monomania, with periodic fits of melancholia. Frequently bursts into tears when crossed. Harsh, guttural voice, and has a habit of raising right hand to shoulder level. DANGEROUS !

Profile from a recent photograph. Black moustache. Jowl inclines to fatness. Wide nostrils. Deep-set, menacing eyes.

FOR MURDER Wanted for the murder of over a thousand of his fellow countrymen on the night of the Blood Bath, June 30, 1934. Wanted for the murder of countless political opponents in concentration camps.

He is indicted for the murder of Jews, Germans, Austrians, Czechs, Spaniards and Poles. He is now urgently wanted for homicide against citizens of the British Empire.

Hitler is a gunman who shoots to kill. He acts first and talks afterwards.

No appeal to sentiment can move him. This gangster, surrounded by armed hoodlums, is a natural killer. The reward for his apprehension, dead or alive, is the peace of mankind.

FOR KIDNAPPING Wanted for the kidnapping of Dr. Kurt Schuschnigg, late Chancellor of Austria. Wanted for the kidnapping of Pastor Niemoller, a heroic martyr who was not afraid to put God before Hitler. Wanted for the attempted kidnapping of Dr. Benes, late President of Czechoslovakia. The kidnapping tendencies of this established criminal are marked and violent. The symptoms before an attempt are threats, blackmail and ultimatums. He offers his victims the alternatives of complete surrender or timeless incarceration in the horrors of concentration camps.

FOR THEFT Wanted for the larceny of eighty millions of Czech gold in March, 1939. Wanted for the armed robbery of material resources of the Czech State. Wanted for the stealing of Memelland. Wanted for robbing mankind of peace, of humanity, and for the attempted assault on civilisation itself. This dangerous lunatic masks his raids by spurious appeals to honour, to patriotism and to duty. At the moment when his protestations of peace and friendship are at their most vehement, he is most likely to commit his smash and grab.

His tactics are known and easily recognised. But Europe has already been wrecked and plundered by the depredations of this armed thug who smashes in without scruple.

FOR ARSON Wanted as the incendiary who started the Reichstag fire on the night of February 27, 1933. This crime was the key point, and the starting signal for a series of outrages and brutalities that are unsurpassed in the records of criminal degenerates. As a direct and immediate result of this calculated act of arson, an innocent dupe, Van der Lubbe, was murdered in cold blood. But as an indirect outcome of this carefully-planned offence, Europe itself is ablaze. The fires that this man has kindled cannot be extinguished until he himself is apprehended—dead or alive !

THIS RECKLESS CRIMINAL IS WANTED—DEAD OR ALIVE!

Propaganda page in the Daily Mirror *published in London on the day after the outbreak of war in September 1939*

EVIDENCE FROM FICTION

Fiction simply means anything which has been invented or made up. Fiction can take many different forms. It includes stories, plays, novels, poems, ballads, rhymes, and the words to songs.

Fiction is often rooted in fact. Authors often base their writings on things they have seen themselves in real life. There is little point in trying to get readers involved in the plot of a story if the descriptions of politicians, ordinary people, houses, shops, working conditions, and clothes of the characters do not ring true as well. The stories are fictional, but the way of life described is usually typical of its time. This can be confirmed by comparing written accounts in novels and stories with factual descriptions, photographs, and pictures.

Fiction also throws light on the way in which people behaved, such as their manners and their customs. It can help us to understand how people spoke and their attitudes to servants or to employers. Descriptions of political events, such as strikes and election meetings, are often particularly vivid because they are written by excellent writers who knew how to make a scene come to life. This is why fiction, including foreign fiction in translation, can be a useful source of historical evidence when studying British, European and modern world history.

Like most historical sources, however, there are drawbacks. If a writer, such as Charles Dickens, felt strongly about an injustice he often exaggerated the problem, or based his story on a particularly bad case (such as the schoolmaster Wackford Squeers in *Nicholas Nickleby*). There is a danger that the writer of fiction may make a particular situation appear to be much worse, or much better, in fiction than it really was in fact.

Going through the Checklist

You can apply the same checks to fiction as you would to a factual historical source. Read the extract opposite describing the start of the battle of El Alamein in 1942. It comes from the novel *The Battle Lost and Won* by Olivia Manning. It was first published in 1978 and forms part of a sequence of six novels. The author did not fight at El Alamein but she knew what she was talking about, since she lived and worked in Egypt and Palestine during the Second World War.

In this short extract British soldiers are awaiting the start of the battle of El Alamein on 23 October 1942 (see also pages 41–2).

The moon, the great white Egyptian moon, rising above the horizon was sharpening every object into sections of silver or black. According to rumour the attack would start at 21.00 hours but 21.00 hours came and went and there was nothing but an expectant silence. The men that remained in the camp had gathered about the command truck, all facing westwards like sightseers awaiting a firework display.

As the brilliance increased, Simon began to feel a fearful impatience, certain that the moon would reveal to the enemy the great concourse of guns and tanks moving towards the tapes. But the night, a windless and quiet night, remained still and, imagining the Germans asleep, he pitied their unsuspecting repose.

Donaldson, making approaches to his seniors, kept looking at his watch and saying knowingly: 'It'll be 22.00 hours, you see if it isn't,' but he was wrong. The barrage started twenty minutes before the predicted time.

It opened with so deafening a roar that some of the men round the truck, a mile or more from the guns, stepped back in trepidation. The timing had been perfect. Every gun had fired on the instant.

[later the same night]

Getting into his sleeping-bag, too tired to notice the noise of the barrage, Simon looked at his watch and saw it was four a.m., the latest he had ever been up in his life. He thought of the ghostly men, each with a white cross on his back, and imagined them still moving through the night. He almost envied them but greater than envy was his desire for sleep.

He was roused two hours later by Crosbie who handed him a mug of tea.

Olivia Manning, *The Battle Lost and Won*
Weidenfeld and Nicolson, 1978

1 *What does the source tell you about the past?*

It describes the start of the Battle of El Alamein on 23 October 1942.

2 *What is the origin of the source? What type of evidence is it? Is it likely to be reliable?*

It is from a novel written by a novelist who was living in Egypt at the time of the battle. El Alamein was only 200 kilometres or so from Cairo and British soldiers often spent their leave there.

3 *Why was the source written?*

As a novel.

4 *When was the source written? Is it a primary source dating from the time of the event which it describes? Or is it a secondary source?*

It was published in 1978, thirty-six years after the Battle of El Alamein. It is probably safer to think of it as a secondary rather than as a primary source, even though it may be partly based on notes made at the time.

Checkpoints 5, 6, 7, and 8 do not apply since this is a work of fiction, not necessarily one of fact.

9 *Are there any obvious mistakes or errors of fact in the extract? Which statements are supported by facts you know about from other sources? Does anything in the extract contradict other sources or facts which you already know to be true?*

We can compare this extract directly with the similar account of the start of the battle on pages 41–2 which was taken from a soldier's diary and gives a real life, day-by-day account of the life of a soldier in an infantry battalion at El Alamein. The comparison reveals two slight discrepancies between the two accounts.
(a) The novelist says it was 'a windless and quiet night'. The soldier says 'A cold wind is blowing in from the sea'.
(b) In the novel the officers appear to be unaware of the time of the gun barrage – 21.40 hours – which signalled the start of the battle – 'According to rumour the attack would start at 21.00 hours ...' But the private soldier appears to have had definite information in advance – 'our barrage is due at twenty to ten'.

10 *Does the account give a distorted view of events which actually occurred? Has the author left out facts which tell a different story?*

No. The account in the novel is substantially the same as the account written by the soldier who fought in the battle.

EXERCISES AND ACTIVITIES

1 *Compare the fictional and factual accounts of the start of the Battle of El Alamein and draw up a list of similarities and differences.*

2 *Which account do you think gives the more vivid impression of the battle?*

FACTS FROM PICTURES

Pictures created shortly after an event are called *contemporary pictures*. Historians often use them as primary sources. They include paintings, sketches, cartoons, drawings, engravings, pictures on pottery, pictures on stamps, pictures on song sheets, statues, carvings, etc.

Many artists use their pictures to say something about the subject they are drawing or painting. The Soviet artist who painted 'Battle for Krukovo Station' (on the outskirts of Moscow) depicts the horrors of war as seen from the point of view of the soldier. 'Rubble in Korea' depicts the horrors of war as experienced by modern civilians.

The Second World War battle for Krukovo Station painted by the Soviet artist A. A. Gorpenko

Rubble in Korea *by
David Hall*

The main drawback to the use of contemporary pictures is that we cannot always be certain that the picture created by the artist actually portrays real things. The concern of many artists in the past was to produce a pleasing picture which was well composed and well drawn or painted. The artist who drew a battle scene often did so from the point of view of one of the participating armies. Since artists have the freedom to emphasize the good or bad points in a scene, two illustrators depicting the same scene or event can sometimes produce two very different pictures.

We cannot always be certain that the pictures we see were actually drawn or painted on the spot or even that they were based on sketches actually made in the field. Some illustrations have been drawn from photographs, or based on newspaper reports and eyewitness accounts. Many detailed and lifelike pictures have been 'imagined' by the artist in a studio. As a consequence we cannot always be sure that realistic pictures of people, places, and events are the eyewitness primary sources they may at first appear to suggest.

A further drawback is that in many cases you will not be able to find out much about the origins of the contemporary pictures you see. This is partly because many pictures have been drawn by anonymous or unknown artists and partly because pictures are often reproduced in books without giving an indication of their actual origin.

Political cartoons based on recent events are another important source of information used by historians studying modern world history. They often sum up a controversy, crisis, or great event in a sketch and a short caption, such as the *Punch* cartoon 'Whose Turn Next?' (below) which depicts Dame Europa warning her pupils (Czechoslovakia, Hungary, Romania, and Poland) that 'The Göblins will get you if you don't watch out!'. As you can see, Austria had already been taken by then (May 1938). This was after the Anschluss (when the Nazis seized power in Austria) but well before the Sudetenland was handed over to Hitler later in the same year (see pages 126–8).

Punch, *18 May 1938*

WHOSE TURN NEXT?

Checklist — **Pictures from the Past**

You will not always be able to answer every checkpoint in this list when you study a picture. This is because most pictures are printed without giving full details of when, where, why, and how they were produced, and by whom.

You can see how each of these checkpoints applies to the pictures on pages 75–7.

1 *Does the picture attempt to portray realistically people, events, buildings, etc., or does it poke fun at them by means of a cartoon or an exaggerated drawing (called a caricature)?*

2 *What does the picture show? What does it tell us about the past?*

3 *When was the picture drawn? Was it drawn at roughly the same time as the event or feature it depicts? Is it a primary source? If no date is given, can you estimate roughly the date when it was drawn from the clothes worn by the people in the picture, from styles of vehicle (such as motor cars), or from other clues?*

4 *Why was the picture drawn or painted? Was it simply an illustration (e.g. to accompany a news item or to illustrate a book) or is there any reason to think the artist was using the picture to make you feel in a certain way about the events or people depicted? For instance, was it drawn or painted to make you want to protest against an injustice, or to feel excited, or sad, or nostalgic for an old way of life, or patriotic, or self-satisfied, or envious of someone else's way of life?*

5 *Does the picture show something which could not be shown in any other way, such as the interior of a courtroom where photographs are not permitted?*

6 *Even if it looks like a realistic picture is there any reason to think it is a product of the artist's imagination rather than a portrayal of an actual scene or event?*

7 *If the picture is a cartoon, what was the artist getting at? What does the cartoon tell you about the topic, events or people portrayed? What does it tell you about the attitude of the artist who drew the cartoon or of the magazine which published it?*

THE FRANCO COMPOSITE AIRCRAFT.

This Punch cartoon points up the fact that Mussolini sent planes to aid General Franco's rebel forces in the Spanish Civil War. Even if we did not know the date of the cartoon – 3 November 1937 – we could probably guess its approximate date from the style of seaplanes shown in the drawing.

Russian poster celebrating the victory of Mao Zedong's Communists in the Chinese Civil War in 1949. What was the purpose of this poster? What did the artist want you to feel about this victory? What do you think the Russian words on the poster mean?

Painting 'A Battery Shelled' by British artist Percy Wyndham Lewis. Compare this picture with the photographs on pages 113–15. What advantages does the artist's picture have over the photographs? Is this a realistic picture or a product of the artist's imagination?

This Punch cartoon which was published on 22 October 1919 celebrates a Red Army defeat and depicts the Bolshevik wolves running for cover. What does this cartoon tell you about British attitudes to the Bolshevik Revolution?

THE RETREAT OF THE RED PACK

Going through the Checklist

SOURCE A

THE OLD MAN OF THE STEPPES.
'We've reached the fifth milestone, little brother,
but the burden isn't any easier yet.'

Cartoon from Punch
*published on 11
January 1933*

1 *Does the picture attempt to portray realistically people, events, buildings, etc., or does it poke fun at them by means of a cartoon or an exaggerated drawing (called a caricature)?*

It is a cartoon which makes fun of the Communist Revolution in the Soviet Union.

2 *What does the picture show? What does it tell us about the past?*

It depicts Josef Stalin, the Russian dictator, riding on the back of a Soviet peasant. Stalin is carrying a hammer and a sickle (the well-known symbol of the USSR) together with a whip. They have just reached the 'fifth milestone' marked with the Roman numeral V on the milestone at the side of a very rough and stony path. Stalin tells the peasant that they have reached the target – the fifth milestone – 'but the burden isn't any easier yet'. This is a reference to Stalin's Five Year Plans which set production targets for industry and for the people. The cartoon shows the attitude of many people in Britain to the Soviet Union at that time.

3 *When was the picture drawn? Was it drawn at roughly the same time as the event or feature it depicts? Is it a primary source?*

It was drawn for the issue of *Punch* dated 11 January 1933. The First Five Year Plan was started in October 1928 and the Second Five Year Plan in November 1933. So it is a primary source.

4   *Why was the picture drawn or painted?*

To make the point that Stalin was not relaxing his grip on the Soviet Union. Life was not to be any easier for the Russians in the next five years either.

Checkpoints 5 and 6 do not apply.

7   *If the picture is a cartoon, what was the artist getting at? What does the cartoon tell you about the events or the people portrayed? What does it tell you about the attitude of the artist who drew the cartoon or of the magazine which published it?*

[See response to checkpoint 2.]

SOURCE B

A scene in Changi Gaol in Singapore where the Japanese kept some of the British and Commonwealth prisoners of war who had been captured when Singapore fell on 15 February 1942. Painted by L. Cole. The prisoners depicted here are suffering from starvation and/or tropical diseases.

1   *Does the picture attempt to portray realistically people, events, buildings, etc., or does it poke fun at them by means of a cartoon or an exaggerated drawing (called a caricature)?*

It is a fairly realistic picture depicting one of the horrors of modern warfare – the prisoner of war camp.

2   *What does the picture show? What does it tell us about the past?*

It conveys a vivid impression of the appalling conditions in which Allied prisoners of war were held by the Japanese during the Second World War.

3   *When was the picture drawn? Was it drawn at roughly the same time as the event or feature it depicts? Is it a primary source?*

No information to hand. It appears to be a primary source.

4 *Why was the picture drawn or painted?*

To highlight the suffering of the prisoners of war who were held by the Japanese in Changi Gaol.

5 *Does the picture show something which could not be shown in any other way?*

Yes – prisoners of war would not have been allowed to keep cameras; so a drawing or painting is the only way in which the horrors of their confinement can be realistically shown.

6 *Even if it looks like a realistic picture is there any reason to think it is a product of the artist's imagination rather than a portrayal of an actual scene or event?*

No.

EXERCISES AND ACTIVITIES

Go through the checkpoints on page 74 with each of the illustrations shown here.

PEACE AND FUTURE CANNON FODDER

The tiger [Clemenceau – with the walking stick]: 'Curious! I seem to hear a child weeping!' Cartoon drawn by William Henry Dyson for the Daily Herald in 1919.

1 *Who are the other people depicted in this cartoon? To which major world event does it refer? What was the point of this cartoon? Why do you think it later achieved great fame?*

Mussolini defied world opinion and the League of Nations when he sent Italian troops to invade Abyssinia in 1935. Some countries wanted to apply sanctions against Italy by cutting off her oil supplies. Others, such as the French Foreign Minister (Pierre Laval) and the British Foreign Secretary (Sir Samuel Hoare), wanted to settle the matter by offering Mussolini a deal he could accept.

2   *Examine this sequence of cartoons from Punch. All were drawn in 1935, the year of the Italian invasion. What do they tell you about the reaction of Abyssinia, of the League of Nations, and of other countries to Mussolini's actions?*

PUTTING BACK THE CLOCK. Punch, *9 October 1935*

THE DUCE HAS DOUBTS. Punch, *13 November 1935*

THE WAR SALAD.

MUSSOLINI. "LET ME SEE—THEY SAY 'A MISER FOR THE VINEGAR, A SPENDTHRIFT FOR THE OIL, AND A MADMAN TO STIR IT.' BUT—IS THE OIL GOING TO HOLD OUT?"

Punch, *11 December 1935*

THE SWEETS OF AGGRESSION.

HAILE SELASSIE. "HAVE I GOT THIS RIGHT?—HE'S TAKEN NEARLY HALF OF WHAT I HAD AND NOW YOU GENTLEMEN WANT TO DISCUSS WHETHER HE SHOULD TAKE ANY MORE!"

Punch, *18 December 1935*

3   *Which cartoon depicts Pierre Laval and Sir Samuel Hoare?*

4   *Which cartoon indicates the problems Mussolini would have faced if oil sanctions had been made effective?*

5   *Which cartoons depict Mussolini, (a) as a Roman Emperor, (b) as a street thug? Why?*

6   *What was the point of this recent cartoon which was drawn by Garland for the Daily Telegraph in 1980?*

Cartoon by Garland in the Daily Telegraph, Thursday, 3 January 1980

FACTS FROM PHOTOGRAPHS

September 1970. A deserted airfield in Jordan. Arab terrorists blow up a British VC10 airliner which had been hijacked on its way to New York. The incident started a civil war in Jordan between Government forces and the Palestinian guerilla forces stationed there.

This remarkable action photograph helps to record the problem posed by international terrorism since the early 1970s. Photographs like this have given historians a new and often very accurate source of evidence. Some of the significant moments of world history have been captured on film, such as the moments before the assassination of the Archduke Ferdinand in 1914 (page 7) or the actual assassination of President Kennedy in 1963 (page 39).

When we look at a photograph we become eyewitnesses to history ourselves. It is true, that in this particular case, we do not see the picture in colour. Nor do we see the movement in the scene or experience the reaction of the onlookers or hear the sound of the explosion. On the other hand, we can study the photograph closely again and again. It is a primary source which a historian can use – either on its own or in conjunction with other sources, such as an onlooker's written or spoken description of the same incident.

Some photographs, like those of the demonstrators in the square in Petrograd in 1917 (page 86), or the air raid on Pearl Harbor in December 1941 (page 89), bring to life a major crisis or world event. It is one thing to read Nikolai Sukhanov's written account of the demonstration in Petrograd (page 9) but the photograph on page 86 gives it a new dimension and helps us to see for ourselves the scale of the challenge which faced the Czar and his officials.

A District Commissioner hears the case against a Sudanese offender at a local court in the Sudan in 1952. Which is the District Commissioner? Which is the offender? How does this scene differ from one in Britain when an offender is brought to court? Do you think it is true that we gave our colonies the same system of justice as in Britain?

Photographs can also be used as sources of information from which we can deduce many other facts about the past. The photograph of the District Commissioner in the Sudan in 1952 helps us to understand how Britain exercised control over a huge colonial Empire by employing local people to maintain law and order. The primitive buildings betray the basic poverty of the area – hence the need to hold the court out of doors despite the hot tropical sun. Note the immaculate white tropical kit of the District Commissioner, contrasted with the clothes of the Sudanese people present at the court hearing.

If you have no precise date for a photograph it is always possible to estimate its date by examining the style of clothes worn by the people in the photograph and also from other pictorial clues, such as makes and types of cars, trams, buses, aeroplanes, and ships.

However, there are some serious drawbacks to the use of photographs as historical evidence. Although a photograph helps you to become an eyewitness to history, it is by no means certain that what you see is a fair representation of reality itself. Photographers select the viewpoints for their photographs. They decide what the photograph will show, *not* the camera! The photograph of the District Commissioner in the Sudan may or may not be typical of similar local outdoor courts throughout the British Empire. Questions like this can only be answered by studying other photographs and by comparing them with pictures and written accounts.

Bear in mind, too, that the camera can also lie. Photographs are sometimes altered to improve the appearance of the people shown in the pictures or to block out something which spoils the view. Some photographs have even been deliberately faked. In *The Independent* for 3 December 1987, Oliver Knox revealed that his cousin

> was in 1964 briefly Chancellor of the Exchequer. Very briefly indeed. The official photograph of the full Cabinet about to be taken, Reginald Maudling was urgently summoned away; and Tony in No. 11 on Treasury business, was press-ganged into deputising – to be decapitated of course when the photograph was printed.

In dictatorships, skilled darkroom assistants have sometimes altered old photographs in order to eliminate a later enemy of the state shown in the earlier photograph to be standing far too close to the Dictator! As you saw on page 28, a poor or unflattering photograph can be printed in a newspaper to try to turn public opinion against a politician.

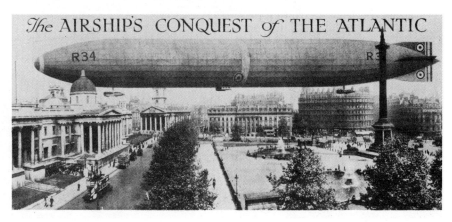

This photograph showing the immense size of the R34 airship was printed in The Graphic *on 12 July 1919. How do you think the photograph was taken?*

Checklist — **Photographs**

1 *What does the photograph show? What does it tell us about the past?*

2 *When and where was the photograph taken? If no date is given use clues to estimate the date.*

3 *Why was the photograph taken? Is there any reason to think the photographer chose a viewpoint or a subject to make us feel in a certain way about the event or people depicted?*

4 *Is there any sign that the people in the photograph are posing for the photographer? Were they aware of the camera? Does this make any difference to the value of the photograph?*

5 *Is there any reason to think that the photograph is not a typical example of what it appears to show? Is there any reason to think that it may have been altered in any way?*

Going through the Checklist

SOURCE A

Photograph showing demonstrators in the square in front of St Isaac's Cathedral in Petrograd during the Russian Revolution in 1917

1 *What does the photograph show? What does it tell us about the past?*

It shows thousands of demonstrators completely packing one of the main squares in Petrograd during the Russian Revolution in 1917 (see page 9). The caption to the photograph does not say whether this was in March, when the Czar was overthrown, or in November, when Lenin and the Bolsheviks seized power. However, the people in the crowd are waving their hats and cheering the person addressing them from a plinth to the left of the statue of the horseman in the centre of the photograph. There are also men in uniform mingling with the crowd. Many Russian soldiers and policemen refused to take action against the demonstrators in the March revolution. The banners look like those carried by the trade unionists and striking workers who protested against bread shortages and against the War in March 1917. But this is not conclusive evidence, many workers also demonstrated in November as well.

2 *When and where was the photograph taken?*

Probably in March 1917 in Petrograd (now Leningrad) but it could have been in November.

3 *Why was the photograph taken? Is there any reason to think the photographer chose a viewpoint or a subject to make us feel in a certain way about the event or people depicted?*

No – apart from a desire to show the immense size of the crowds of demonstrators. Judging by the high viewpoint above the crowd, the photographer may have been standing on the plinth of another statue in order to take the photograph.

4 *Is there any sign that the people in the photograph are posing for the photographer? Were they aware of the camera?*

Crowds of this size do not pose for photographers. Almost all are engrossed by the stirring events of the day. Only one or two people can be seen looking towards the camera.

5 *Is there any reason to think that the photograph is not a typical example of what it appears to show? Is there any reason to think that it may have been altered in any way?*

No.

SOURCE B

Photograph showing Russian and American soldiers meeting at Torgau on the Elbe in April 1945

1 *What does the photograph show? What does it tell us about the past?*

It shows American soldiers on the left and Russian soldiers on the right shaking hands. The photograph shows clearly that forward units of the two great Allied armies – the Red Army from the East and Eisenhower's Army from the West – had completely encircled Germany. It was only a matter of days before Germany was defeated.

2 *When and where was the photograph taken?*

On or about 27 April 1945 at Torgau (near Leipzig) on the river Elbe in what is now East Germany.

3 *Why was the photograph taken? Is there any reason to think the photographer chose a viewpoint or a subject to make us feel in a certain way about the event or people depicted?*

The photograph was obviously taken to symbolise the linking up of the two great Allied armies. It gives every indication of having been carefully posed to enable the photographer to create an interesting and striking picture. After fighting their way across Europe, however, you might have expected these soldiers, especially the Russians, to embrace each other in the style of soccer players after a goal has been scored! Instead they shake hands! Did the photographer want us to feel a slight chill between the two armies?

4 *Is there any sign that the people in the photograph are posing for the photographer? Were they aware of the camera?*

What do you think?

5 *Is there any reason to think that the photograph is not a typical example of what it appears to show? Is there any reason to think that it may have been altered in any way?*

No.

EXERCISES AND ACTIVITIES

1 *Use the checklist on page 85 to help you study the two photographs printed opposite.*

2 *Both photographs have been reprinted many times. Why? What was their value to the Americans as propaganda in the war against the Japanese?*

3 *What is the value of these photographs, if any, to the historian of the Second World War?*

Pearl Harbor, 7
December 1941

On the summit of
Mount Suribachi on
the Pacific island of
Iwo Jima, 23 February
1945

4   Use the checklist on page 85 to check out the photograph below showing Lenin in 1921. What does this photograph tell you about Lenin?

'Lenin Beating the Bolshevik Drum'. From The Graphic, 13 August 1921. The caption in the magazine read as follows: 'A recent portrait of the Russian dictator appealing to soldiers in a public square in Moscow to remain banded together "for the glory and safety of Russia" – that Russia which under the tyrannic Bolshevik régime, has been transformed into a desolation in which now stalk abroad the twin monsters, Famine and Disease.'

EVIDENCE IN SOUND AND ON FILM

The first sound recordings were made by Thomas Alva Edison in 1877. The first moving films were made in the 1890s. These two great inventions provided historians with important new sources of evidence. Since they are not in printed form, however, their value in the study of history has not always been appreciated. Only since the coming of television has effective use been made of old film for the benefit of the general public. As a result people can now see movie film of the funeral of Queen Victoria in 1901 or watch the coronation of Queen Elizabeth II in 1953. Old movie films enable us to see or hear some of the events of history as they happened.

The main drawback to the use of movie film is that it can be easily edited (altered) to show whatever the film editor wants us to see. Lengths of movie film can be cut out and then stuck back together in a different order. It is very easy to assume that because the images are moving in a documentary film we are actually seeing events in sequence exactly as they happened at the time. In many cases you are, but you cannot be certain of this! Movie film has been one of the most powerful weapons used by people involved in propaganda (as in Nazi Germany) and in advertising (see also pages 64–7).

On pages 22–4 you saw evidence relating to the tragic death of Emily Wilding Davison after the Epsom Derby on 4 June 1913. A movie film was made of the race and shown at the Palace Theatre in London. This is how a journalist on *The Times* described the film when he saw it shown for the first time on Derby night, 1913.

The tragic incident at the 1913 Derby

A CINEMATOGRAPH VIEW

The scene at Tattenham Corner was shown on the cinematograph at the Palace Theatre last night. Viewed from a point opposite Tattenham Corner the vast crowd was seen with every head turned in the direction from which the horses were coming. A moment later a bunch, so closely packed that it is scarcely possible to distinguish one horse from another, passed at a great pace. There is a pause for a moment, and suddenly a woman is seen to spring forward from behind the white rails, but as she sets foot upon the course two horses come by. There is a flicker and a flash of white, the woman is prostrate on the turf and a jockey is flung head foremost from his mount and lies in a huddled heap a dozen yards from the woman. A moment more and the remaining horses have passed, but the jockey and the woman lie still and silent, and then the great crowd, moved by a common impulse, closes round them.

The Times, Thursday, 5 June 1913

As it happens, we can see this film ourselves, since the clip of film described in this report has been shown several times on television. It has also been included in at least one schools' television broadcast.

Immediately after the incident, some eyewitnesses said that Emily Wilding Davison deliberately tried to stop the race but others thought that she had mistakenly assumed the race was over and was trying to get to the other side of the racecourse. To the eyewitnesses at Epsom, glued to the race, the incident, which was over in a flash, came as a complete and unexpected shock. It was unthinkable that anyone would actually want to run on to the track during the race. Not surprisingly, they had different versions of what happened in the midst of the confusion.

The modern viewer of this movie film when seen on a video recorder has no such excuse for not knowing exactly what happened! Slow motion and the rewind button can be used to get an instant replay of history! In other words you can be an eyewitness to an important historical event, but with the added advantage of being able to repeat the film over and over again until you think you know for sure what happened.

Almost every historian who has ever described this event in print (including the author until he saw the video recording of a schools broadcast!) is on record as saying that Emily Wilding Davison 'threw herself under the King's horse'. This is because everyone later assumed that this is what must have happened, since she was a suffragette and presumably wanted to bring the cause of the suffragettes to the notice of the world. What better way to do this than by throwing herself in front of the King's horse to disrupt the most famous horse race in the world?

Here, instead, is a modern 'eyewitness' account of the 1913 Derby written after watching about a dozen replays of this incident on a video recorder.

Emily Wilding Davison can be seen clearly ducking under the barrier after the leading horses have passed. She stands upright in the middle of the racecourse, facing the remaining horses in the race. Her arms appear to be stretched outwards. At no time does she fling herself under the hooves of a horse. She seems bewildered, at first, trying to grab at the reins of three horses all close together and passing her far too quickly for her to have any chance of stopping them. Then there is a short gap in the field. It is enough to give her the chance to position herself and reach up to the next horse as it races towards her. She grabs at the reins again but is knocked down and the horse and jockey also fall. Two other horses ride past as they lie on the ground.

In other words, the 'cinematograph film' proves conclusively that:

- Emily Wilding Davison did not throw herself under the hooves of the King's horse. Far from it. She was standing upright all the time and her only motion when the horse approached was to reach up with her hands towards the reins.
- It was sheer chance that the horse that knocked her down was Anmer, the King's horse. In fact, she tried to stop the earlier horses as soon as she stepped on to the race track.
- Anmer was third from last at Tattenham Corner. It was *not* leading the field, nor was it the last horse in the race. This corrects the misleading statements in Sources A (page 22) and D (page 23).

These may seem trivial points but they do have some importance to the history of the suffragette movement. In the first place they suggest that Emily Davison did not really set out to become a martyr at all although she did want to stop or disrupt the race. In fact she gives every impression of having been taken aback by the speed of the horses. So perhaps she was not quite the heroine and martyr portrayed by the suffragettes in their subsequent literature. Equally she was not the 'half demented' woman depicted by many commentators and historians both at the time and since.

EXERCISES AND ACTIVITIES

Look closely at clips of old newsreel film on a video recorder or whenever an old documentary film is shown on schools television. Use your eyes and ears to note carefully what happens. Record your observations as an eyewitness would have done had he or she been a witness to the same event.

If possible take the opportunity to view the film of the 1913 Derby. Write your own 'eyewitness' account of the incident and compare it with those printed above.

FACTS FROM STATISTICS

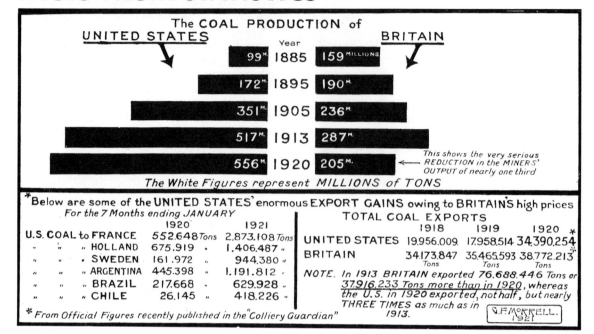

The COAL PRODUCTION of

UNITED STATES   Year   BRITAIN

United States	Year	Britain
99ᴹ	1885	159 MILLIONS
172ᴹ	1895	190ᴹ
351ᴹ	1905	236ᴹ
517ᴹ	1913	287ᴹ
556ᴹ	1920	205ᴹ

This shows the very serious ←— REDUCTION in the MINERS' OUTPUT of nearly one third

The White Figures represent MILLIONS of TONS

*Below are some of the UNITED STATES' enormous EXPORT GAINS owing to BRITAIN'S high prices

For the 7 Months ending JANUARY

	1920	1921
U.S. COAL to FRANCE	552,648 Tons	2,873,108 Tons
" " " HOLLAND	675,919	1,406,487 "
" " " SWEDEN	161,972	944,380 "
" " " ARGENTINA	445,398	1,191,812 "
" " " BRAZIL	217,668	629,928 "
" " " CHILE	26,145	418,226 "

TOTAL COAL EXPORTS

	1918	1919	1920
UNITED STATES	19,956,009	17,958,514	34,390,254
BRITAIN	34,173,847 Tons	35,465,593 Tons	38,772,213 Tons

NOTE. In 1913 BRITAIN exported 76,688,446 Tons or 37,916,233 Tons more than in 1920, whereas the U.S. in 1920 exported, not half, but nearly THREE TIMES as much as in 1913.

G.F.MORRELL. 1921

* From Official Figures recently published in the "Colliery Guardian"

Why do you think this graph and the statistics underneath were published in The Graphic *on 14 May 1921 at the time of a coal miners' strike? What were these statistics designed to show? How did they affect two of the main developments of the 1920s – the 'Boom and Bust' years in the United States and the General Strike in Great Britain?*

Statistics are an important source of information for the historian. The most important sources of statistics in British history are the official census reports which have been published every ten years since the first Census in 1801. Official statistics of wartime casualties, army recruitment, agricultural and industrial production, length of railway line, numbers of people unemployed, and countless other statistics have also been published. Statistics like these are invaluable since they help us to measure the effect of war, the progress or decline of industries, and the growth or decline of towns.

But there are problems. Some statistics can mislead. They may have been collected or counted in circumstances which led to inaccuracies. The first census reports were compiled from census returns, completed by householders, many of whom were illiterate. Sometimes the statistics are biased. They may be incomplete.

Many printed statistics, like opinion polls, are based on samples, instead of being complete surveys. Statistics for 1930 tell us about 1930. These may or may not be typical of the 1930s as a whole. Statistics for London tell us about London, not about the rest of Britain. Unfortunately, you will rarely have the chance to check for yourself when, how, why and where the statistics were collected and whether they are reliable.

This is why it is best to treat all statistics with a certain amount of caution and to use them as a guide rather than as proof. In particular, beware of believing statistics just because they back up your own or other people's arguments!

Checklist — **Statistics**

1 *When and how were the statistics collected? Who collected them? Were they in a position to collect accurate or reliable statistics? Can we be certain they are not guesses, estimates, approximations, or even lies?*

2 *Is it likely that someone else working in exactly the same way would collect the same statistics? If not, why not?*

3 *Are the statistics complete or only a sample of all the possible statistics which could have been recorded?*

4 *Who selected the statistics for use and how were they chosen?*

5 *What do the statistics tell you about the past? What do they prove? If they are quoted to back up a statement do they really support the conclusions drawn from them by the writer?*

6 *Are the statistics used to support a statement which may be biased or prejudiced?*

7 *If averages are used do they mean anything? See if you can find out how they were calculated.*

Going through the Checklist

This German grocer needed a tea chest to hold the day's takings in 1923!

The statistics printed below show the decline in the value of the German paper mark compared with the value of gold in the period between January 1919 and November 1923. A gold mark was worth 1.97 paper marks in January 1919. A year later it was worth 19.86 paper marks. In other words, the value of the paper mark fell to only a tenth of its former value in the course of twelve months. Ten times as much paper money was needed to buy the same amount of gold in January 1920 as in January 1919. This was an inflation rate of about 1000 per cent.

	1919	1920	1921	1922	1923
January	1.97	19.86	14.40	47.89	1167
February	2.18	23.93	14.97	54.17	3405
March	2.48	17.38	14.87	72.62	4994
April	3.04	13.63	15.74	67.38	7096
May	3.09	8.87	15.06	65.95	16 550
June	3.33	9.17	17.89	89.17	36 790
July	3.59	10.12	19.20	159.52	261 900
August	4.60	11.85	20.56	410.71	2 453 000
September	5.81	14.82	27.50	392.86	38 100 000
October	6.50	18.21	42.98	1071.00	17 261 000 000
November	9.29	16.85	58.33	1821.00	1 000 000 000 000
December	11.47	17.47	43.81	1750.00	

Heinz Huber and Artur Muller, *Das Dritte Reich*, Verlag Kurt Desch, 1964

1 *When and how were the statistics collected? Who collected them?*

Like most published statistics we have little information on this. They may have been calculated by a German bank or by a Government department.

2 *Is it likely that someone else working in exactly the same way would collect the same statistics?*

No. The sweeping changes from month to month in 1922–3 must mean that different figures would have been shown had the statistics been collected on the 1st, 15th, or 30th of each month, or as an average of each month.

3 *Are the statistics complete or only a sample of all the possible statistics which could have been recorded?*

They are only a sample since the statistics could have been recorded week by week or even day by day.

4 *Who selected the statistics for use and how were they chosen?*

No information — but we can only assume that the statistics were collected in the same way each month.

5 *What do the statistics tell you about the past? What do they prove? If they are quoted to back up a statement do they really support the conclusions drawn from them by the writer?*

The statistics show that inflation was a serious problem in Germany in 1919 as well as in the later years. The value of the mark dropped to only a tenth of its former value between January 1919 and January 1920. It dropped to only a fortieth of its former value between December 1921 and December 1922 and to a thousandth of its former value between June and September 1923. By then it was virtually worthless.

6 *Are the statistics used to support any statement which may be biased or prejudiced?*

No.

EXERCISES AND ACTIVITIES

1 *Draw a graph to show the rise and fall of the German mark:*
   (a) in the three years from 1919 to 1921,
   (b) in 1922,
   (c) in 1923,
   (d) for all five years.
   What do you notice after studying the graphs you have drawn? Did the value of the mark decline at a steady rate? Did it always fall in value throughout the entire period of almost five years? In which year was the value of the mark most erratic? Write a paragraph describing the problem of inflation in Germany in the five years before December 1923.

2 *Study the statistics on the next page showing the rise and fall of share prices on the New York Stock Exchange between January 1925 and December 1933.*
   (a) Use the checklist to test these statistics.
   (b) When do you think the Great Wall Street Crash occurred?
   (c) When was the best time to buy stocks and shares before the Great Wall Street Crash?
   (d) When was the best time to buy stocks and shares after the Great Wall Street Crash?
   (e) When was the best time to sell stocks and shares before the Great Wall Street Crash?
   (f) When was the best time to sell stocks and shares after the Great Wall Street Crash?

3 *Draw a graph to show these statistics.*

	1925	1926	1927	1928	1929	1930	1931	1932	1933
January	83	102	106	137	193	149	103	54	46
February	84	102	108	135	192	156	110	53	43
March	81	96	109	141	196	163	112	54	42
April	80	93	110	150	193	171	100	42	49
May	83	93	113	155	193	160	89	38	65
June	85	97	114	148	191	143	87	34	77
July	88	100	117	148	203	140	90	36	84
August	89	103	120	153	210	139	89	52	79
September	92	104	129	163	216	139	76	56	81
October	96	102	128	166	194	118	65	48	76
November	100	103	131	179	145	109	68	45	77
December	100	105	136	178	147	102	54	45	79

(NB These are the average prices you would have had to pay for stocks or shares worth 100 dollars in July 1926.)

Histoire d'une guerre à l'autre (1914–1939), Hachette, 1982

Worried investors gather in Wall Street after the Great Wall Street Crash in 1929 when the value of stocks and shares suddenly fell, making thousands of people bankrupt

Working as a Historian

SIMILARITIES AND DIFFERENCES

German barbed wire entanglements in 1916

Allied barbed wire entanglements in 1916. In both cases the barbed wire was strung up to protect a concealed trench immediately behind the wire. Compare the two pictures. Can you pick out the trenches? What similarities are there? How do the two scenes differ from each other?

From *Sir Douglas Haig's Great Push*, Hutchinson

Similarity does not mean 'the same'. It means that things are alike in certain respects but not identical. This is an important difference. Two mill towns may look alike to an outsider but they may be very different places to the people who actually live there.

In fact, every historical event is unique. There is nothing quite like it. This is why it is often much easier to detect differences than it is to find similarities. Nonetheless, there are patterns in history. A revolution in one country may be followed by similar revolutions in neighbouring countries.

If you are asked to look for similarities or differences in history you may be asked to compare two or three written extracts or a number of pictures or photographs. You will need to pick out the important things that matter, not the minor details. If you jot down the main similarities and differences first of all, you can use these lists later on to help plan your essay.

EXERCISES AND ACTIVITIES

Study Sources A, B, C, D and the photographs. They show how people greeted the outbreak of the First World War in London and Berlin.

SOURCE A

A JOURNALIST IN LONDON

AUG: (Piccadilly Hotel) Was awakened by loud noises. Great crowds are parading the streets, exulting in the anticipation of war. This mafficking [rejoicing] for such universal tragedy makes me feel sad, and I am unable to sleep. Wasn't it Walpole who said: 'Yes! they are ringing their bells now; soon they will be wringing their hands!'? . . . I cannot sleep. They are going mad. Have they no imagination? They say war with Germany is inevitable. Possibly so – but why jubilate [rejoice] – how *can* they? . . . Can they not realise what war really means, these mad maffickers – what it means to women as well as men?

The Private Diaries of Sydney Moseley, Max Parrish, 1960

SOURCE B

A LONDON NEWSPAPER

A lady came out of the Palace, and announced that war had been declared. This was received with tremendous cheering, which grew into a deafening roar when King George, Queen Mary and the Prince of Wales appeared on the balcony shortly after eleven o'clock.

They looked down upon an extraordinary scene – a dense mass of excited people, many of whom had clambered on to the Victoria Memorial. As if by general accord, the cheers gave way to the singing of the National Anthem, which was taken up lustily by the whole throng.

For fully five minutes the Royal Party remained on the balcony. They retired amidst a perfect storm of cheering, and although the crowd subsequently began to melt away, thousands remained. They grew gradually less demonstrative, and it was noticeable that the news of the actual state of war had a sobering effect on many. Mafficking gave way to distinct seriousness.

Daily News and Leader, 5 August 1914

Crowds outside Buckingham Palace. London, August 1914

Crowds in the Unter den Linden. Berlin, August 1914

SOURCE C

A BRITISH JOURNALIST IN BERLIN

For two days I waited and watched. Up and down the wide road of Unter den Linden crowds paced incessantly by day and night singing the German war songs: 'Was blasen die Trompeten?' [Who blows the trumpet?] which is the finest; 'Deutschland, Deutschland ueber Alles,' [Germany, Germany above all] which comes next, and 'Die Wacht am Rhein,' [The Watch on the Rhine] which was the most popular . . . Sometimes the Kaiser in full uniform swept along in his fine motor . . . Cheered he was certainly, but everyone believed or knew that the Kaiser himself had never wished for war . . . The most mighty storm of cheering was reserved for the Crown Prince, known to be at variance with his father in longing to test his imagined genius on the field. Him the people cheered, for they had never known war.

Henry W. Nevinson, *More Changes, More Chances*, James Nisbet, 1925

SOURCE D

A BRITISH WOMAN IN BERLIN

BERLIN, August 9th, 1914.

The excitement and enthusiasm all over the city are enormous. The Kaiser is the most adored man of the moment, and during a great speech he delivered the other day on the balcony of the castle, in spite of the people standing densely thronged together, the silence was so great that one might have heard a pin fall. Certainly the whole nation are backing him this time, and if he has been criticized for his actions in the past, this war-cry is making him the most popular man in Germany.

Evelyn, Princess Blücher, *An English Wife in Berlin*,
Constable, 1921
[She and her German husband had been living in
England but returned to Germany on 6 August 1914.]

1   *Use the master checklist on page 51 to check out these sources first of all. Are they primary sources? Are they eyewitness accounts? Which parts of these extracts are facts and which are opinions?*

2   *What were the similarities and differences between Berlin and London in the way in which people greeted the war? How do you account for the similarities? Is that how people always greet a declaration of war?*

3   *Do any of the writers appear to be biased or prejudiced? The descriptions of Berlin were written by people who were British not German. Is there any sign that this may have affected the way in which they described the reactions of the Germans to the war?*

4   *Do the photographs support or contradict the written sources? In what ways are these photographs similar?*

5   *Do the written sources support or contradict each other?*

6   *Do you think you have enough information to be able to say how people, in general, greeted the outbreak of war in August 1914?*

The accounts which follow also describe scenes at the outbreak of the First World War but in Buxton, a small English country town (Source E) and in a village near the French fishing port and holiday resort of Morlaix in Brittany (Source F).

SOURCE E

BUXTON, ENGLAND

Wednesday, August 5th

The town was quite quiet when we went down, though groups of people were standing about talking & one or two Territorials [part-time soldiers] were passing through the streets. Several Territorials & one or two Reservists were going off by train this morning &

there was a small crowd on the station seeing them off. Close by us a Reservist got into a carriage & his father & a girl, probably his wife, came to say goodbye. The girl was crying but they were all quite calm ... Though excitement & suspense are wearing, I felt I simply could not rest but must go on wandering about.

Vera Brittain, *Chronicle of Youth*, Victor Gollancz, 1981

SOURCE F

A BRETON VILLAGE NEAR MORLAIX, FRANCE

It was Saturday afternoon [2nd August]. Everybody was waiting in the streets. The beach was empty. At midday the news had already gone round that the order for mobilization would arrive any moment. I went once more to the post office to enquire ...

About half-past two the clerk of the Mairie arrived on a bicycle, with ceaseless bell-ringing, from the direction of Morlaix. He was hugging a black portfolio under his arm. The mobilization order.

> [Mobilization meant that many of the men in the town would be called up immediately to serve in the French army in case war broke out against Germany. It did – the next day – 3 August].

At three o'clock the tocsin [alarm] shrieked. The senseless clanging of the village church bell was a worthy heralding of the world's gloomy change ...

Old women in black with white head-dresses came hurrying. Suddenly they were all over the space round the platform which had been set up in front of the church, like big, white-crested, black birds. Then the men, as many of them as were at home, arrived in their Sunday clothes.

The holiday-makers silently made way for the assembling villagers. They had first right to hear the news.

In deathly silence the mayor read out the order for general mobilization.

Then petrified dumbness. Not a voice applauded. Someone sobbed, once, and the crowd stirred, and everyone went their various ways home.

Aladar Kuncz, *Black Monastery*, Chatto & Windus

5 *Use the master checklist on page 51 to check out Sources E and F. Are they primary sources? Are they eyewitness reports? Which parts of these extracts appear to be facts and which are opinions?*

6 *Make a list of the ways in which the events depicted in these two extracts are similar to each other and how they differ from Sources A to D.*

7 *Which of the six extracts do you think you would pick if you had to choose one to read out at a Remembrance Day ceremony?*

SOURCE G

Cover of the German
magazine Jugend, issue
no. 3 published in
1916

SOURCE H

Cartoon in Punch in
March 1916
commemorating the
epic battle at Verdun
in which over 200,000
French soldiers were
killed

TO THE GLORY OF FRANCE.

8 *What are the similarities and differences between Sources G and H?*

9 *What is the link between Source G and Source C?*

10 *How did the artist who drew Source G expect the German people to
react to his picture? How did the Punch artist expect people in Britain to
react?*

11 What was the point of the two cartoons below? Why were they drawn?

12 What are the similarities between these two cartoons?

Russian propaganda cartoon in 1919 showing the Western Allies controlling the commanders of the three main White Armies (Denikin, Kolchak, and Yudenich). The White Armies were fighting the Red Army in the Russian Civil War. You can see a reference to the White Armies in the extract printed on page 31.

German propaganda cartoon from the Second World War – ENTENTE CORDIALE – showing Churchill (left), Stalin (centre) and Roosevelt (right)

HOW THINGS CHANGE

These photographs show how rapidly things can change. In 1945 Cologne, Essen, Düsseldorf, Frankfurt, Hamburg, Munich, Berlin and many other German cities had been reduced to ruins as a result of Allied air raids. Yet within fifteen years most had recovered and German industry was thriving once again. The Germans called it the Wirtschafts-wunder – the 'economic miracle'. Only Japan rivalled Germany in her ability to recover from defeat and destruction at the end of the war – as you can see in the diary extract on page 62.

Cologne in 1945

Cologne today

How and why things change is of great interest to historians. Sometimes the changes are abrupt and clear-cut, such as the sudden change in policy which happens when a revolutionary government seizes power. Changes of equal or greater significance in the lives of ordinary people also take place but often slowly over periods of many years.

Despite these changes many things, such as people's attitudes, customs and traditions, often remain much the same. This is called continuity. Change and continuity can both be identified when you make comparisons over a period of time.

Checklist — **Change**

Use these checkpoints if you are asked to identify changes which may have taken place.

1 *What was the nature of the change? Was it part of a much bigger change?*

2 *Was it an important and significant change? Did it affect everybody and almost every activity, like a political change, such as a revolution or a radically different government? Or did it just affect a section of the community, such as the effect of the means test in the 1930s on the unemployed?*

3 *Who or what benefited from the change? Who or what suffered from the change?*

4 *Did the change take place suddenly, rapidly, steadily, slowly, jerkily, or imperceptibly?*

5 *Did the change affect people mainly because of its political effects, such as its effect on relations with other countries? Or because of its social and economic effects, such as on health or on industry?*

Going through the Checklist

BERLIN

November 8, 1918
I wonder what the result of the meeting of the delegates for an armistice today will be? . . . Every one expects that France will take her fill of revenge and make terms as hard as she can. Poor Germany is not in a position to resist any humiliation; she is completely exhausted.

Evening, November 9, 1918
Gebhardt and I were sitting quietly reading our papers, when at about two o'clock a perfect avalanche of humanity began to stream by our windows, walking quietly enough, many of them carrying red flags . . .

Our butler came in to announce that the Kaiser had abdicated. Tears came into both our eyes as we grasped the momentousness of the hour . . . But it was not time to mourn for the individual, and our attention was soon fixed on what was passing outside our windows. There, evidently no one sorrowed at the loss of an emperor. There could hardly have been a greater air of rejoicing had Germany gained a great victory. More and more people came hurrying by, thousands of them densely packed together – men, women, soldiers, sailors . . .

Sunday morning, November 10, 1918
After we had all separated for the night, I lay awake, very tired. We were constantly disturbed by the sound of stray rifle-shots, and the feeling of uncertainty as to what was going on out there in the darkness of the huge city made sleep impossible . . .

Princess Taxis rang us up to say that the new Socialist Chancellor, Ebert, has already threatened to resign as he cannot hold the people . . . Amongst the aristocracy the grief at the breakdown of their country, more than at the personal fall of the Kaiser, is quite heart-rending to see. I have seen some of our friends, strong men, sit down and sob at the news, whilst others seemed to shrink to half their size and were struck dumb with pain.

Evelyn, Princess Blücher, *An English Wife in Berlin*,
Constable, 1921

German soldiers waving red flags and driving through the centre of Berlin in November 1918

Compare the extract above with the same writer's description of Berlin and the Kaiser at the start of the war only four years earlier (Source D on page 102).

1   *What was the nature of the change? Was it part of a much bigger change?*

It was a catastrophic change. Germany was exhausted; the armistice was about to be signed; the abdication of the Kaiser had brought to an end the Prussian monarchy and the German Empire. Germany was now a socialist republic. There was a very real possibility of a communist revolution, following the example of the Bolsheviks in Russia a year earlier.

2   *Was it an important and significant change? Did it affect everybody and almost every activity, or just a section of the community?*

Obviously it was an important and significant change, affecting everybody living in Germany. The autocratic rule of the Kaiser was at an end. No one knew what sort of government would take its place. The Princess Blücher was most disturbed at the uncertain future which lay ahead.

3   *Who or what benefited from the change? Who or what suffered from the change?*

The ordinary people, soldiers, sailors, strikers obviously thought that they would benefit. The aristocracy assumed that they would suffer and that their world had come to an end. The Princess Blücher described their 'grief at the breakdown of their country' and said that their reaction was

> quite heart-rending to see. I have seen some of our friends, strong men, sit down and sob at the news, whilst others seemed to shrink to half their size and were struck dumb with pain.

4   *Did the change take place suddenly, rapidly, steadily, slowly, jerkily, or imperceptibly?*

Suddenly with the collapse of the German war effort. The abdication of the Kaiser obviously came as a great shock – 'Tears came into both our eyes as we grasped the momentousness of the hour'.

5   *Did the change affect people mainly because of its political effects? Or because of its social and economic effects?*

Mainly because of its political effects at the time. It was too early to say what the social and economic effects would be.

EXERCISES AND ACTIVITIES

This Russian propaganda comic strip was published in *The Graphic* on 29 May 1920, less than three years after the start of the Bolshevik Revolution in Russia in November 1917.

PETER WORKED HARD ON HIS CORNFIELD

WHILE VASSILY WAS DRUNK BOTH NIGHT AND DAY

Just at this time there fell upon Russia a great misfortune – the régime of the Soviet.

A SOVIET ORATOR ARRIVED ON THE SCENE

AND FOR VASSILY THERE CAME A HIGH OLD TIME

BUT PETER WAS VERY HARDLY DEALT WITH

When a Leninite orator came down the drunken and ragged Vassily was the most enthusiastic of those present at the meeting, and was rewarded by being the first to receive authority over the village ... Vassily proclaimed the socialisation of property, and carried off all poor Peter's belongings.

*AND THIS IS WHAT HAPPENED TO THE VILLAGE AFTER
A MONTH OF THE BOLSHEVIK REGIME*

The result was that while some of the inhabitants deserted the village with their children, others lay in the cold grey earth. It was decreed that whoever had worked all his life with industrious hands was a harmful man. The cattle died and only the Soviet Committee and the dogs had enough to eat. Thus did the Bolshevik Vassily rule. While these pictures may be exaggerated, the story told in words is not; it is an accurate description of what has been happening all over Russia since the country had the tragic misfortune to fall under the tyranny of its new rulers. The people live under a perpetual Reign of Terror without parallel in Russian history. Murder stalks abroad in the land. Outrages are committed everywhere. The industrial life of the great nation has been paralysed. Famine has been added to the horrors of the people. Nothing is deemed sacred by the authors of this prolonged orgy of fiendish misrule.

The Graphic, 29 May 1920

1   *Examine this propaganda strip with the aid of the checklist for bias and prejudice on page 29. In particular, examine the way in which it was used by The Graphic.*

2   *What changes did the Bolshevik Revolution have on Russia according to the authors of this propaganda strip? Use the checklist printed on page 107 to examine these changes.*

3   *Find out what really happened to agriculture in Russia in the first three years under communism. Was there any truth whatsoever in the propaganda strip? Was it 'an accurate description of what has been happening all over Russia since the country had the tragic misfortune to fall under the tyranny of its new rulers'?*

4   *What do you think the Russian cartoonist was getting at in the picture below? What change had taken place? In what ways is it similar to the 1920 comic strip on page 110–11?*

Cartoon in the Soviet Union's humorous magazine Krokodil, *the Russian equivalent of* Punch. *The cartoon was drawn in 1952.*

IMAGINING THE PAST

Trying to imagine what it was like to live in the past is called historical *empathy*. It is a way of trying to understand why people behaved in the past in the way they did. Instead of judging their actions by our own standards we look at events and happenings through the eyes of the people living at that time.

Really understanding what happened in the past will only come about if you can set aside your own ideas and background and picture yourself in the past. How would you have behaved then? A good way to imagine yourself in the past is to think of everything in the present tense! What are your thoughts (in 1956) as you watch the Russian tanks rumble through the streets of Budapest? Describe your feelings (in 1968) as you demonstrate against the Vietnam War outside the White House in Washington.

Another way of getting a vivid picture of what it was like to live in the past is to read accounts and stories which tell you how people spoke and how they behaved. Look closely at old pictures and especially at old photographs. When you see a photograph of the Sharpeville Massacre in 1960, for instance, try to imagine what it must have been like to take the picture or to be in the crowd.

EXERCISES AND ACTIVITIES

Look at the following sources on trench warfare in the First World War (see also pages 77 and 99).

SOURCE A

Inside a trench

SOURCE B

'A Working Party'

Three hours ago he blundered up the trench,
Sliding and poising, groping with his boots;
Sometimes he tripped and lurched against the walls
With hands that pawed the sodden bags of chalk.
He couldn't see the man who walked in front;
Only he heard the drum and rattle of feet
Stepping along barred trench boards, often splashing
Wretchedly where the sludge was ankle-deep.

Voices would grunt 'Keep to your right – make way!'
When squeezing past some men from the front line:
White faces peered, puffing a point of red;
Candles and braziers glinted through the chinks
And curtain-flaps of dug-outs; then the gloom
Swallowed his sense of sight; he stooped and swore
Because a sagging wire had caught his neck.

A flare went up; the shining whiteness spread
And flickered upward, showing nimble rats
And mounds of glimmering sand-bags, bleached with rain;
Then the slow silver moment died in the dark.
The wind came posting by with chilly gusts
And buffeting at corners, piping thin.
And dreary through the crannies; rifle-shots
Would split and crack and sing along the night,
And shells came calmly through the drizzling air
To burst with hollow bang below the hill.

Siegfried Sassoon

SOURCE C

A LETTER FROM THE WESTERN FRONT

4 July 1916   B.E.F. [British Expeditionary Force]
From BOSKY   France

Am in a very comfortable DUG OUT with heaps of Head cover,
which is a great change from GALLIPOLI. But the mud is awful.
Have had two days of Torrential Rain which has flooded
everything. And the RATS ARE A CAUTION. I didn't believe
there were so many in the country. Black as well as brown. In fact
I'm fed up with the war. French life in France is not what it is
cracked up to be. . . .

My Warrior Sons, edited by Guy Slater,
Peter Davies 1973

SOURCE D

*A bombing party off to
the attack*

SOURCE E

A LETTER HOME

December 14, 1916
According to the present routine, we stay in the front line eight
days and nights; then go out for the same period. Each Company
spends four days and four nights in the fire-trench before being
relieved. The men are practically without rest. They are wet
through much of the time. They are shelled and trench-mortared.
They may not be hit, but they are kept in a perpetual state of unrest
and strain. They work all night and every night, and a good part of
each day, digging and filling sandbags, and repairing the breaches
in the breastworks; – that is when they are not on sentry. The
temperature is icy. They have not even a blanket. The last two days
it has been snowing. They cannot move more than a few feet from
their posts: therefore, except when they are actually digging, they
cannot keep themselves warm by exercise; and, when they try to
sleep, they freeze. At present they are getting a tablespoon of rum
to console them, once in three days.

Rowland Feilding, *War Letters to a Wife*,
The Medici Society, 1929

SOURCE F

A British officer leading his section over the top on the first day of the battle of the Somme, 1 July 1916

SOURCE G

'The Sentry'

We'd found an old Boche dug-out, and he knew,
And gave us hell, for shell on frantic shell
Hammered on top, but never quite burst through.
Rain, guttering down in waterfalls of slime,
Kept slush waist-high and rising hour by hour,
And choked the steps too thick with clay to climb.

Wilfred Owen

SOURCE H

Painting from The Sphere *for 5 August 1916 showing a British officer leading his section across no man's land towards the enemy trenches*

1   *Use the checklists on pages 51, 74 and 85 to check through these extracts and the accompanying pictures.*

2   *Imagine that you are a soldier fighting in the trenches in 1916. What do you look like? What clothes are you wearing? When did you last wash or eat? What can you smell, see and hear? What is it like to live in a trench for several days at a time? What do you feel like when it is pouring with rain, or when it is hot in summer? What is it like in the middle of the night? What is it like in icy weather or when there is heavy snow? What do you feel like before making a raid across the lines in the middle of the night? What is it like 'to go over the top'? Describe your life in the trenches in a series of letters home.*

3   *Write a diary for a week in the life of a suffragette in June 1913 (see pages 22–4 and 91–3).*

CAUSE AND CONSEQUENCE

Nazi propaganda against the Jews. Young children shown reading Der Stürmer, a viciously anti-Jewish newspaper edited by the notorious Julius Streicher. How have the Jewish people been depicted here?

Buchenwald Concentration Camp. What cause and what consequence are illustrated in these pictures?

Whenever we look at how things change (see pages 106–12), we also look at the causes and consequences of making those changes. Scientists in subjects such as physics and chemistry can usually find out for certain why a change occurs. They can repeat an experiment over and over again until they are satisfied with the result. As a result, they know that if they repeat the cause (such as adding sulphuric acid to zinc) they will always get the same result or consequence (zinc sulphate and hydrogen). In history there is no such certainty.

Politicians argue that in appearing to give in to Hitler at Munich in 1938 (see pages 126–8), the British prime minister, Neville Chamberlain, only encouraged the Nazis to invade Poland in 1939. A policy like this, of giving way to a dictator, is called *appeasement*. Munich has since been used as a reason for acting toughly today. In other words, many politicians believe that aggression is the inevitable consequence of a policy of appeasement.

In fact, the Munich Crisis was unique. It is by no means certain that a similar consequence would follow in different circumstances, with another dictator, at another date, in another country. History is not like that. It can show people what happened in the past. It can teach them to learn from their past mistakes. But it cannot lay down strict laws like those you may have learned in science. You can see this illustrated in the cartoon.

THE GAP IN THE BRIDGE

The consequence indicated by this cartoon in *Punch* on 10 December 1919 was the founding of the League of Nations. The cause was the ambition and enthusiasm of the US President, Woodrow Wilson, who wanted to create a common meeting place – the League of Nations – where the countries of the world could settle their disputes peacefully around the conference table instead of on the battlefield. Wilson thought it so important, he insisted that the Treaty of Versailles should include a Covenant setting up the League of Nations. But despite his enthusiasm there was an unpredictable outcome. Many of his fellow Americans favoured a policy of isolationism instead. They did not want the United States to become involved in world problems. On 19 November 1919, the US Senate refused to agree to the terms of the Treaty of Versailles, precisely because it would have meant that the United States would have had to join the League of Nations. The *Punch* cartoonist, like most people in Europe, felt that the world had been let down by the United States. The League – or 'bridge' between nations – had indeed been 'designed by the President of the USA' but the 'keystone' country – the United States – never joined.

Checklist — **Cause and Consequence**

Use these checkpoints when you study cause and consequence.

1   *What are the suggested effects and consequences?*

2   *Are these effects and consequences facts which can be proved or disproved? Or are they opinions?*

3   *What causes of these effects and consequences have been given?*

4   *Which of these causes can be backed up by facts and evidence? Can they be proved or disproved?*

Going through the Checklist

Exactly what was the real cause of the war no one seems to know, although it is discussed night and day. One thing grows clearer to me every day: neither the people here nor there [in Britain] wished for war, but here they are now being carried off their legs with patriotism, at seeing so many enemies on every side. It is said in England that Germany provoked the war, and here they emphatically deny it. To me it seems that Europe was thirsting for war, and that the armies and navies were no longer to be restrained. Certainly here, the militarists grew weary of the long lazy peace as they called it, and if the Kaiser had not proclaimed war, he would have been in a precarious position.

Evelyn, Princess Blücher, *An English Wife in Berlin*, Constable, 1921

1   *What are the suggested effects and consequences?*

The outbreak of the First World War.

2   *Are these effects and consequences facts which can be proved or disproved? Or are they opinions?*

Facts.

3   *What causes of these effects and consequences have been given?*

That the militarists in the armies and navies of Europe were thirsting for war and could no longer be restrained. In other words, that the arms race was a major cause of the war.

4   *Which of these causes can be backed up by facts and evidence? Can they be proved or disproved?*

It is easy enough to quote facts which show the extent of the arms build-up before 1914 but it is not easy to show that this is the reason why war broke out. That some people welcomed the chance to go to war has already been shown in the extracts and photographs on pages 100–2.

EXERCISES AND ACTIVITIES

The following sources all relate to the dropping of the first atomic bombs on Hiroshima (6 August 1945 – 80 000 people killed) and on Nagasaki (9 August 1945 – 40 000 people killed). Japan surrendered on 15 August 1945.

The atom bomb exploding above Nagasaki on 9 August 1945

SOURCE A

It was hard to believe what we saw ... We dropped the bomb at exactly 9.15 a.m. and got out of the target area as quickly as possible to avoid the full effect of the explosion. We stayed in the target area two minutes. The smoke rose to a height of 40,000 feet [12,000 metres] ... We knew at once we had to get the hell out of there. I made a sharp turn in less than half a minute to get broadside to the target. Nothing was visible where only minutes before there was the outline of a city, with its streets and buildings and piers clearly to be seen.

Colonel Paul Tibbits, captain and pilot of the
Enola Gay, the American Superfortress bomber
which dropped the first atomic bomb.
[*Daily Mail*, Wednesday, 8 August 1945]

SOURCE B

AUGUST 8, 1945

Eye-witness accounts of the effect of the first atomic bomb – dropped on Hiroshima, a Japanese city of over 300,000 inhabitants – were received from Guam.

Captain William Parsons of the United States Navy, who observed the attack from the Superfortress which dropped the bomb, said:

'When the bomb fell away, we began putting as much distance between us and the ball of fire which we knew was coming as quickly as possible. There was a terrific flash of light, brilliant as the sun. That was the first indication I had that the bomb worked.'

Each man gasped. What had been Hiroshima was going up in a mountain of smoke.

'First I could see a mushroom of boiling dust apparently with some debris in it up to 20,000 ft. [6,000 metres]. The "boiling" continued for three or four minutes as I watched. Then a white cloud plumed upwards from the centre to some 40,000 ft. [12,000 metres].

An angry dust cloud swirled and spread all round the city. There were fires on the fringes of the city, apparently burning as buildings crumbled and gas mains broke.'

The *Daily Telegraph*, Wednesday, 8 August 1945

SOURCE C

Dr Michihiko Hachiya worked in a hospital in Hiroshima. He described the explosion in his diary on Monday 6 August 1945:

Scorching winds howled around us, whipping dust and ashes into our eyes and up our noses. Our mouths became dry, our throats raw and sore from the biting smoke pulled into our lungs. Coughing was uncontrollable ...

The streets were deserted except for the dead. Some looked as if they had been frozen by death while in the full action of flight; others lay sprawled as though some giant had flung them from a great height.

Michihiko Hachiya, *Hiroshima Diary*, translated by Warner Wells

SOURCE D

Ron Bryer, a British prisoner of war, was forced to work in the dockyard at Nagasaki.

He was standing in a small trench in Nagasaki on August 9, 1945, and he watched the atom bomb come down half a mile away ... We've read all about Schultz and Shevardnadze [the US and Soviet foreign ministers] and their deliberations in Geneva but Bryer knows more about the effects of a nuclear war than the rest of them put together ...

At about three minutes past the hour [11.03 a.m.], Bryer looked out and saw a large plane flying in over the sea. Suddenly there was a mighty crescendo of noise, like engines over-accelerating. The plane turned and departed, leaving a bomb suspended from three parachutes which drifted slowly down ...

The violet liquid flash lasted for a long time. There was no explosion – just a series of rocking vibrations. ... A rushing wind swept debris over him. He blacked out ... It was pitch black, except for the moving pin-pricks of people on fire. No noise. No screaming. ... Everything he saw was on silent fire. Telegraph posts burning from the top down, vegetables frying in the fields, and, away down to the left, every ship in the harbour alight ...

'After what seemed a long, long time, with the sun now up at its high point and all the earth hot and burning, the first real emotion, the first thing I can remember, now slowly coming into my mind, was shame. I started to feel guilty. I looked at my clean hands and felt ashamed.'

Russell Harty in the *Sunday Times*, 29 November 1987

SOURCE E

The atom bomb was no 'great decision' . . . It was merely another powerful weapon in the arsenal of righteousness. The dropping of the bombs stopped the war, saved millions of lives.

President Truman

1   *With each of the five sources A, B, C, D, E, go through the master checklist printed on page 51 and the checklist printed on page 119.*

2   *Are the reported consequences the same in each case? Is the reported cause the same in each case? How do you account for these differences?*

The ruins of the Japanese city of Hiroshima after the dropping of the world's first atom bomb

SELECTING RELEVANT INFORMATION

Selecting relevant information means selecting only those facts, opinions, judgements and ideas which relate specifically to the subject you are studying.

It is interesting to know that Florence Nightingale was called Florence because she was born in Florence in Italy. But this information is irrelevant if you are studying her work as a nurse. It is relevant, however, if you are writing the story of her life. It is easy to be sidetracked in this way. This is why you should always try to make an effort to stick to the subject. Use only information which throws light on your topic.

EXERCISES AND ACTIVITIES

In 1916 a group of Irish Republicans, led by Patrick Pearse, attempted to seize power in Dublin on Easter Monday, 24 April. They declared Ireland a Republic but the revolt was put down within a week. Eamon De Valera, a commandant in the Easter Rising, later went on to become leader of Sinn Fein and, in 1921, President of the Dail Eireann, the Irish Parliament. In December 1921, he, and other Republicans, declared their opposition to the Treaty signed by Irish representatives in London which was to establish the Irish Free State a year later in December 1922.

1   Read the three sources below and then list the relevant clauses in the Treaty to which you think he and the other Irish Republicans probably objected.

SOURCE A

POBLACHT NA H EIREANN.

THE PROVISIONAL GOVERNMENT
OF THE
IRISH REPUBLIC
TO THE PEOPLE OF IRELAND.

IRISHMEN AND IRISHWOMEN : In the name of God and of the dead generations from which she receives her old tradition of nationhood, Ireland, through us, summons her children to her flag and strikes for her freedom.

Having organised and trained her manhood through her secret revolutionary organisation, the Irish Republican Brotherhood, and through her open military organisations, the Irish Volunteers and the Irish Citizen Army, having patiently perfected her discipline, having resolutely waited for the right moment to reveal itself, she now seizes that moment, and, supported by her exiled children in America and by gallant allies in Europe, but relying in the first on her own strength, she strikes in full confidence of victory.

We declare the right of the people of Ireland to the ownership of Ireland, and to the unfettered control of Irish destinies, to be sovereign and indefeasible. The long usurpation of that right by a foreign people and government has not extinguished the right, nor can it ever be extinguished except by the destruction of the Irish people. In every generation the Irish people have asserted their right to national freedom and sovereignty ; six times during the past three hundred years they have asserted it in arms. Standing on that fundamental right and again asserting it in arms in the face of the world, we hereby proclaim the Irish Republic as a Sovereign Independent State, and we pledge our lives and the lives of our comrades-in-arms to the cause of its freedom, of its welfare, and of its exaltation among the nations.

The Proclamation of the Republic by the leaders of the Easter Rising, 24 April 1916. As you can see, it explains the reasons for the rebellion and the aims of the Irish Republican Brotherhood.

SOURCE B

months from the date hereof.

18.   This instrument shall be submitted forthwith by His Majesty's Government for the approval of Parliament and by the Irish signatories to a meeting summoned for the purpose of the members elected to sit in the House of Commons of Southern Ireland, and if approved shall be ratified by the necessary legislation.

Dec 6th 1921.

On behalf of the British Delegation

D. Lloyd George

Austen Chamberlain

Birkenhead.

Winston S. Churchill

On behalf of the Irish Delegation

Ayr Ó Gríobhthá (Arthur Griffith)

Mícheál Ó Coileáin (Michael Collins)

Riobárd Bartún (Robert Barton)

(E. J. Duggan)

(Gavan Duffy)

Last page of the peace treaty granting home rule to the Irish Free State – dated 6 December 1921. The British signatures (on the left) include those of David Lloyd George and Winston Churchill. The Irish signatures (on the right), include those of Arthur Griffith and Michael Collins, leaders of the first Free State government.

SOURCE C

Extracts from the Treaty establishing the new Irish Free State.

(1)   Ireland shall have the same constitutional status in the ... British Empire as the Dominion of Canada, the Commonwealth of Australia ... with a Parliament having powers to make laws for peace and order and good government in Ireland ... and shall be styled and known as the Irish Free State.

(2) The position of the Irish Free State [in relation to the UK] ... shall be that of the Dominion of Canada ...

(3) A representative of the Crown in Ireland shall be appointed in like manner as the Governor General of Canada ...

(4) The oath to be taken by the members of the Parliament of the Irish Free State shall be in the following form:
'I do solemnly swear true faith and allegiance to the Constitution of the Irish Free State as by law established, and that I will be faithful to his Majesty King George V, and his heirs and successors by law.'

(6) Until ... the Irish Free State undertakes her own coastal defence, defence by sea of Great Britain and Ireland shall be undertaken by his Majesty's imperial forces ...

(16) Neither the Parliament of the Irish Free State nor the Parliament of Northern Ireland shall make any law so as to either directly or indirectly to endow any religion or prohibit or restrict the free exercise ... of religious belief ...

2 *Eamon De Valera said the Treaty made 'British authority our masters in Ireland'. Some of his fellow Republicans called it 'A Free State that's tied up with Red, White and Blue'. Why?*

FOR AND AGAINST

A *reasoned argument* is one in which each stage of the argument follows from the preceding one. It uses good reasons to argue the case for or against. The reasons are good because they are based on known facts rather than on bias, prejudice or inaccurate facts.

Use this checklist when you examine the arguments in any historical source.

Checklist — A Reasoned Argument

1 *List the arguments* for.

2 *List the arguments* against.

3 *Which of these arguments are based on facts and which are opinions? Which can be proved? Which are unprovable?*

4 *Which arguments seem to you to be backed up by the most convincing evidence? Which arguments are weak and unconvincing? Which side has the better case?*

EXERCISES AND ACTIVITIES

The brief extracts that follow are just some of the many different opinions which were expressed in the two or three days immediately following the signing of the Munich Peace Agreement on 30 September 1938.

1 *Examine the arguments carefully and then list them in two columns – the arguments for and the arguments against.*

2 *Which of the arguments used by the supporters and opponents of the Munich Agreement are based on facts and which are opinions? Which arguments do you think could be supported by proof? Which are unprovable?*

3 *Which arguments seem to you to be backed up by the most convincing evidence? Which arguments are weak and unconvincing? Which side has the better case?*

4 *How would you have reacted to the Munich Agreement on 1 October 1938?*

Londoners digging trenches in preparation for war – September 1938

SOURCE A

... the settlement is only putting off the evil day ...

Letter in *Daily Herald*

SOURCE B

Who'll trust us? It's like throwing your own kid to the wolves. We helped make it a country and then Chamberlain comes along and wants to buy that swine off. There'll be a war sooner or later, then there'll be nobody to help us.

London bus conductor

SOURCE C

So it is peace, and a Chamberlain, respectable gentleman's peace: the whole world rejoices whilst only a few malcontents jeer.

Sir Henry Channon – a Conservative MP

SOURCE D

... the German dictator, instead of snatching his victuals from the table, has been content to have them served to him course by course ... we have sustained a defeat without a war

Winston Churchill – a Conservative MP

SOURCE E

The peace of Munich has left us less strong than we were yesterday, since we have lost an ally, and more than 30 German divisions will be available to be turned against us. If we were incapable of resisting the formidable German menace in the past when we were stronger, how will we resist the next time when we will be less strong?

French newspaper – *L'Epoque*

SOURCE F

They [the Germans] are being enriched by a territory [the Czechoslovak Sudetenland] abundantly provided and marvellously equipped.

French newspaper – *Le Figaro*

SOURCE G

The Munich agreement has done better than put aside war. It has brought back into the hearts of all the love of peace and has shown in a striking fashion that the most difficult problems can henceforward be resolved round a table.

French newspaper – *L'Oeuvre*

SOURCE H

Let no man say too high a price has been paid for peace in Europe until he has searched his soul and found himself willing to risk in war the lives of those who are nearest and dearest to him.

New York Times

SOURCE I

There is little now to prevent Hitler from dominating and organising Middle and Eastern Europe.

Chicago Tribune

SOURCE J

The Nobel Prize should be awarded to Mr. Chamberlain. The whole world agrees that nobody ever did more for peace. The prize was created for men like him.

Norwegian newspaper – *Tidens Tegn*

SOURCE K

Britain and France have consented under a threat of war to give Germany control of important and strategic industrial areas.

Sydney Morning Herald

SOURCE L

Mr. Chamberlain's great victory is that he won the fight for a civilised system of settling big issues around the council table and not on the battlefield.

Montreal Star

SOURCE M

The Prime Minister has confidence in the good will and in the word of Herr Hitler, although when Herr Hitler broke the Treaty of Versailles he undertook to keep the Treaty of Locarno, and when he broke the Treaty of Locarno he undertook not to have further territorial aims in Europe. When he entered Austria he authorized his henchmen to give an authoritative assurance that he would not interfere with Czechoslovakia, and that was less than six months ago.

Duff Cooper – a Government Minister who resigned
from the Cabinet in protest at the signing of the
Munich Agreement

SOURCE N

He [Hitler] has successfully divided and reduced to impotence the forces which might have stood against the rule of violence . . . Today we are in a dangerous position. We are left isolated. All potential allies have gone . . .

Clement Attlee [Labour Party] –
Leader of the Opposition

SOURCE O

Owing to her geographical position, if war had come, whoever won or lost, Czechoslovakia would have been inevitably destroyed with immense slaughter and devastation.

Sir Samuel Hoare – Home Secretary

SOURCE P

. . . there were, he maintained four hopeful features. For the first time a dictator had made some concession. Again, dictators had learned that hatred of war prevailed among their own well-drilled peoples. . . . Thirdly, in spite of Dr. Goebbels, the German people now knew that Britain too wanted peace; and lastly, there was a great awakening in this country to the need that conciliation must be backed by strength [i.e. rearmament].

Report of speech by Sir John Simon –
Chancellor of the Exchequer

REACHING A CONCLUSION

In an examination, or in a special study, you will often have to reach a conclusion. This is a summing up of what you know about a topic. A good conclusion will balance different opinions and arguments against each other and then state clearly the verdict of the writer. A good conclusion will be supported by facts and historical evidence (if this is available). It will avoid making generalisations based on only one or two examples.

EXERCISES AND ACTIVITIES

1 *Examine the sources A, B, C, D, and E which follow, testing each with the checklist printed on page 51. In particular, take note which are primary and which are secondary sources.*

2 *Source A below was written at the end of 1916. In it Sir Douglas Haig, the commander of the British army, sums up the results achieved in the battle of the Somme, the world's bloodiest battle. Use Sources B, C, D, and E which follow, to say why you agree or disagree with his conclusion. In particular, check each of his 'three main objects' against the facts quoted by the other sources.*

3 *Write your own conclusion, based on Sir Douglas Haig's statement, but correcting it in the light of the information you obtain from these other sources.*

SOURCE A

By the third week in November the three main objects with which we had commenced our offensive had already been achieved: Verdun had been relieved; the main German forces had been held on the Western Front; and the enemy's strength had been very considerably worn down. 'Any one of these three results,' writes Sir Douglas Haig, 'is in itself sufficient to justify the Somme battle. The attainment of all three of them affords ample compensation for the splendid efforts of our troops and for the sacrifices made by ourselves and our Allies. They have brought us a long step forward towards the final victory of the Allied cause.'

Sir Douglas Haig's Great Push, Hutchinson
(No date given but almost certainly early in 1917.)

SOURCE B

It is claimed that the battle of the Somme destroyed the old German Army by killing off its best officers and men. It killed off far more of our best and of the French best.

David Lloyd George, *War Memoirs*, Odhams Press, 1933
(British Prime Minister from 1916 to the end of the war)

*Field Marshal Sir
Douglas Haig in 1916*

SOURCE C

The battle with the greatest recorded number of military casualties was the First Battle of the Somme, France from 1 July to 19 Nov 1916, with 1,043,896 – Allied 623,907 (of which 419,654 were British) and 419,989 German.

Guinness Book of Records 1987

SOURCE D

In the Somme fighting of 1916 there was a spirit of heroism which was never again found in the division . . . the men in 1918 had not the temper, the hard bitterness and spirit of sacrifice of their predecessors.

From *Die 27 Infanterie Division im Weltkrieg*, the Official History of the German 27th Infantry Division

SOURCE E

. . . at a conference on February 14th, an agreement was reached by which Haig accepted Joffre's plan for the Somme offensive – dated for July 1st . . . the offensive was only a few weeks old when the story was spread . . . that Haig was throughout aiming at a campaign of attrition [wearing down the enemy] and had not dreamt of a 'breakthrough'. This denial was vehemently maintained for years, long after the war; it forms one of the most elaborate perversions of historical truth that has come to light . . . publication of the Official History in 1932 . . . revealed that . . . Haig . . . both sought and believed in a breakthrough.

B. H. Liddell Hart, *History of the First World War*, Cassell, 1970

Notes

(a) A 'campaign of attrition' means wearing the enemy down – you lose soldiers but expect the enemy to lose even more.
(b) The battle of Verdun was fought between French and German armies from 21 February to 16 December 1916.
(c) The frontline at the end of November 1916 was still much the same as it had been on 1 July 1916. The battle of the Somme had little effect in hastening the end of the war, which did not come until two years later in November 1918.

Summary Checklists

Master Checklist — Documentary Evidence

1 *What does the source tell you about the past?*

2 *What is the origin of the source? What type of evidence is it (e.g. diary, letter, newspaper report)? Is it likely to be reliable?*

3 *Why was the source written? Was it written to justify the writer's actions? Does the writer try to take credit for successes which other people claim for themselves? Does the writer put the blame for failures on to other people?*

4 *When was the source written? Is it a primary source dating from the time of the event which it describes? Or is it a secondary source?*

5 *Is there any clue or statement to show that it is an actual eyewitness account? Was the writer in a good position to say what happened? Does the source agree with other eyewitness accounts of the same event? Are there any reasons for thinking the eyewitness cannot be trusted entirely?*

6 *If the source was written years after the event is there any reason to doubt the accuracy of the writer's memory?*

7 *Which parts of the extract seem to you to be opinions and not facts which can be proved right or wrong? Are the opinions based on facts or on prejudice? Has the writer used words of approval or disapproval, or colourful or exaggerated phrases, to try to influence the reader?*

8 *Does the author show any other signs of bias or prejudice? Does the writer appear to take sides in an argument?*

9 *Are there any obvious mistakes or errors of fact in the extract? Which statements are supported by facts you know about from other sources? Does anything in the extract contradict other sources or facts which you already know to be true?*

10 *Does the account give a distorted view of events which actually occurred? Has the author left out facts which tell a different story? Is any part of the extract an obvious lie or exaggeration? Are there any obvious gaps in the evidence, such as missing dates, facts, or personalities?*

Checklist — Pictures from the Past

1   Does the picture attempt to portray realistically people, events, buildings, etc., or does it poke fun at them by means of a cartoon or an exaggerated drawing (called a *caricature*)?

2   What does the picture show? What does it tell us about the past?

3   When was the picture drawn? Was it drawn at roughly the same time as the event or feature it depicts? Is it a primary source? If no date is given, can you estimate roughly the date when it was drawn from the clothes worn by the people in the picture, from styles of vehicle (such as motor cars), or from other clues?

4   Why was the picture drawn or painted? Was it simply an illustration (e.g. to accompany a news item or to illustrate a book) or is there any reason to think the artist was using the picture to make you feel in a certain way about the events or people depicted? For instance, was it drawn or painted to make you want to protest against in injustice, or to feel excited, or sad, or nostalgic for an old way of life, or patriotic, or self-satisfied, or envious of someone else's way of life?

5   Does the picture show something which could not be shown in any other way, such as the interior of a courtroom where photographs are not permitted?

6   Even if it looks like a realistic picture is there any reason to think it is a product of the artist's imagination rather than a portrayal of an actual scene or event?

7   If the picture is a cartoon what was the artist getting at? What does the cartoon tell you about the topic, events or people portrayed? What does it tell you about the attitude of the artist who drew the cartoon or of the magazine which published it?

Checklist — Relics from the Past

1   What was the purpose of the object or building you are studying? What was it used for? Why was it built or made?

2   Can you date the object or building either exactly or approximately?

3   Where is it situated now or where was it found? Where did it come from originally?

4   What does it tell us about people in the past?

Checklist — **Photographs**

1   What does the photograph show? What does it tell us about the past?

2   When and where was the photograph taken? If no date is given, use clues to estimate the date.

3   Why was the photograph taken? Is there any reason to think the photographer chose a viewpoint or a subject to make us feel in a certain way about the event or people depicted?

4   Is there any sign that the people in the photograph are posing for the photographer? Were they aware of the camera? Does this make any difference to the value of the photograph?

5   Is there any reason to think that the photograph is not a typical example of what it appears to show? Is there any reason to think that it may have been altered in any way?

Checklist — **Statistics**

1   When and how were the statistics collected? Who collected them? Were they in a position to collect accurate or reliable statistics? Can we be certain they are not guesses, estimates, approximations, or even lies?

2   Is it likely that someone else working in exactly the same way would collect the same statistics? If not, why not?

3   Are the statistics complete or only a sample of all the possible statistics which could have been recorded?

4   Who selected the statistics for use and how were they chosen?

5   What do the statistics tell you about the past? What do they prove? If they are quoted to back a statement do they really support the conclusions drawn from them by the writer?

6   Are the statistics used to support a statement which may be biased or prejudiced?

7   If averages are used, do they mean anything? See if you can find out how they were calculated?

Checklist — Change

1   *What was the nature of the change? Was it part of a much bigger change?*

2   *Was it an important and significant change? Did it affect everybody and almost every activity, or just a section of the community?*

3   *Who or what benefited from the change? Who or what suffered from the change?*

4   *Did the change take place suddenly, rapidly, steadily, slowly, jerkily, or imperceptibly?*

5   *Did the change affect people mainly because of its political effects, such as on relations with other countries? Or because of its social and economic effects, such as on health or on industry?*

Checklist — Cause and Consequence

1   *What are the suggested effects and consequences?*

2   *Are these effects and consequences facts which can be proved or disproved? Or are they opinions?*

3   *What causes of these effects and consequences have been given?*

4   *Which of these causes can be backed up by facts and evidence? Can they be proved or disproved?*

Checklist — A Reasoned Argument

1   *List the arguments* for.

2   *List the arguments* against.

3   *Which of these arguments are based on facts and which are opinions? Which can be proved? Which are unprovable?*

4   *Which arguments seem to you to be backed up by the most convincing evidence? Which arguments are weak and unconvincing? Which side has the better case?*

Checklist — **The Link with the Past**

1 *Find out if there are any features, such as buildings, monuments, street names, or house names near your home which link up in some way with the topic.*

2 *Which of your living relatives were alive for part of the time covered by the topic? What do they remember about this period?*

3 *What things from the past can you find in your local museum or library which link up with this topic?*

Index

CONCEPTS, SKILLS, AND SOURCES

THEMES IN MODERN WORLD HISTORY